Managing in China

Dedication

To my friends in Shanghai and Beijing who have made *Managing in China* possible for me (in both senses of the word 'managing'), particularly JC, NL and SZ.

Managing in China

An Executive Survival Guide

Dr Stephanie Jones

Butterworth-Heinemann Asia,
an imprint of Reed Academic Publishing Asia,
a division of Reed Elsevier (Singapore) Pte Ltd
1 Temasek Avenue
#17-01 Millenia Tower
Singapore 039192

ISBN 9810080867

Cover design by Fred Rose
Typeset by Keyword Editorial Services
Printed by International Press Co (Pte) Ltd

Foreword

When I first came to China in 1980, it was a different world. The first joint venture of Deng Xiaoping's new leadership had just been signed, but virtually no-one, even in Hong Kong, was thinking then of China's business potential. Just coming here was a desperately bureaucratic affair. China's mental and physical exhaustion, not to mention its financial and creative bankruptcy, legacies of the Cultural Revolution and the Gang of Four, was visible everywhere. It was anybody's guess in which direction China was heading.

No-one imagined that less than 20 years later China would be receiving foreign direct investment of almost US$40 billion in one year—more than anywhere else except the United States. No-one dreamt that China would be a formidable economic tiger in its own right, nor that this could be achieved by the same Communist government responsible for all the errors of the previous 40 years.

Foreword

This unparalleled business revolution under Communism has brought many challenges, not least of which is that of business management for foreign companies. This challenge is, above all, a human one. In the same multinational office today you might find Europeans, Americans (perhaps American-born Chinese), Taiwanese, Hong Kong and South-East Asian Chinese, as well as mainland Chinese of different generations and from different parts of the country. All have different experiences of and attitudes to China, and all have very different cultural and educational backgrounds (not to mention varying levels of skill in Mandarin).

How then does one create a happy working atmosphere where everyone strives for more or less the same corporate goals? While this may seem a difficult enough task, contemplate the problems confronting a joint venture, where the foreign investor is often seen by the local partner as an arrogant aggressor imposing on him its own unsuitable and alien ideas and products. Conversely, the foreign partner may well regard the local partner as handicapped by overemployment, poor management, lack of commercial direction, inadequate marketing and clapped-out machinery.

The potential for misunderstanding is enormous and is partly the result of China's long isolation and lack of education. Anything that can be done to improve mutual understanding is valuable, and Dr Stephanie Jones's book—born of her own experiences and those of others—is especially so.

Everyone, overseas Chinese or big-nosed foreigner alike, tends to imagine the frustrations they sometimes feel in China are unique. They seldom are. Stephanie Jones looks at a range of problems and ways to understand them better and, perhaps through that, to understand ourselves better.

Managing in China will be useful to anyone doing business here, for the management challenges are simply changing, not getting any easier. The potential for success here will mean that more and more foreign businesses *have* to deal with China.

I imagine that before long there will be a counterpart to this book in China, probably called *Managing Foreigners*. For just as we study China, so the Chinese need to study us. Perhaps Stephanie Jones's next challenge will be in writing such a book—in a joint venture.

RICHARD GRAHAM
14 January 1997

Richard Graham is head of ING Barings in China; Director, ING Baring Securities (HK) Ltd.; Director (Institutional Group), Baring Asset Management; Director, The Greater China Fund Inc.; Chairman, The British Chamber of Commerce Shanghai; and was formerly British Trade Commissioner China.

Contents

Contents

Part Three
Managing in China: Important working relationships

Part Four
Managing in China: Your personal life

Preface

The process of writing *Managing in China* has actually helped me manage more successfully over the last year and a half of living in the PRC. I regard the title as having a double meaning: on the one hand, 'managing in China' encompasses the job of managing local staff and, to a lesser extent, the presence or absence of resources, while on the other hand, it concerns managing oneself, and coping with the challenges and trials of living and working in China. The task of interviewing many kindred spirits and putting all this down in writing has been both illuminating and therapeutic. I have learnt to manage in China in both senses of the word.

China is certainly the fastest-growing and exciting market to be working in right now, and probably the most difficult for expatriates to live in. Many *laowei* (foreigners) think it must be much easier for overseas Chinese, while many expats of Chinese origin feel it must be easier to be a *laowei*. No-one finds it easy. It all depends on your understanding of the situation and attitude to the job in hand.

After many years closed off from the rest of the world, China has opened up with a vengeance, and is now growing too quickly, too soon. It is experiencing all the problems attendant upon a new economic power emerging in an environment where centuries of development are trying to blend all at once. Where else can you buy compact laser discs where the price is calculated by abacus? Where mothers hang washing in the trees while their children log on to the Internet? And where the authorities struggle to maintain control over the thinking and values of a vast population of over a billion people who are being bombarded by overseas media and foreign consumer products?

Reed Academic Publishing have ambitious plans for a series of practical books aimed at helping managers in different markets, and they recognized the need for such a book on China. Inevitably, I haven't been able to cover all aspects of 'managing in China'. Singapore, where this book is published, is the home of many China hands, as are Hong Kong, Taiwan and elsewhere. I have tried to write this book for the benefit of both overseas Chinese and Westerners and while writing it, in fact, interviewed more overseas Chinese than Westerners to compensate for the fact that I'm a Westerner myself. But I'm sure that Western biases creep through.

While I have tried to include the insights of executives from a variety of industries and sectors, I've tended to concentrate more on those expats who come to work for multinational companies, rather than those who set up in China as entrepreneurs or work for local Chinese companies—although I would hope that there is material of interest here for them, too.

As I'm based in Shanghai and travel frequently to Beijing, and as I know both Hong Kong and Taiwan fairly well, my sources tend to be from those places. I have not covered the lives of expatriates in the wilds of China, as I've had no opportunity to visit them. This book has been written in spare moments during the pursuit of a busy executive career, and is very much the result of on-the-job experiences in China's capital and leading commercial city. Those executives far from 'civilization' deserve their own *Managing in China* book, and I would be gratified if this tome inspires a similar effort from one such person.

Impressions and experiences of working and living in such a *different* place as China are deeply personal and subjective, but I've tried to be neither unduly critical nor unquestioningly positive about the insights I've gained during my time here. It is enough to say that I feel committed to staying here much longer, that my learning curve is still extremely steep, and that I find every day just as challenging and exciting as the last.

Dr Stephanie Jones
Shanghai
May 1997

Acknowledgments

The author is indebted to the many people who gave generously of their time to share insights on and information about their experiences living and working in China. Without their help, this book could not have been written. The reader will find it useful to know something about the background of the principal interviewees, and the following are biographical notes.

Ms **Kathy Bao**, an ambitious and resourceful Taiwanese businesswoman, has been coming to China on-and-off since 1992, '...and now it's mostly "on" as I'm here more than half of my time,' she explains. Her retail outlet, the Sunrise Department Store, close to Shanghai's Sheraton Hua Ting Hotel, was the first foreign-invested retail operation permitted in Shanghai when it opened in 1992; it was preceded by a wholesale business founded in 1990 that dealt solely in underwear.

Sunrise, a chain of department stores in Taiwan, was acquired in 1974 by Chung Shing Textile Company, a business founded in Taiwan by Bao's father, C.Y. Bao. Originally a native of Jiangsu Province, just north of Shanghai, he moved to Shanghai when he was 18 years old and started his business there, fleeing 20 years later to Taiwan in the wake of the Communist takeover. There he started his business again from scratch, taking in all the processes, including finishing and dyeing, becoming an integrated textile company. He concentrated first on underwear and then on knitwear. The Chung Shing businesses in Taiwan are now nearly 50 years old.

C.Y. Bao's daughter Kathy was born in Taiwan and entered the family business in Taipei before coming to Shanghai to manage the store here, together with a colleague from Taipei who is also permanently based in Shanghai. The business broke even by the end of its first year and made a profit from the beginning of its second year. Mr C.Y. Bao unfortunately passed away before he could fulfil his dream of returning to China. However, the company's plan was carried into effect by his widow, who runs the entire Chung Shing operation from Taipei.

Sunrise in China, a high-end store (although much more mass market than the parent company in Taiwan), has the potential to be the flagship of the company and stores are being planned for Beijing, Tianjin and other major cities. The company has its head office in Shanghai and already has five factories and seven branch offices, in retailing, manufacturing and distribution, with a total of 22 joint ventures in China. Twenty-eight Taiwanese managers are based in China.

Mr **Alan Chieng**, assistant food and beverage manager at the Swissotel in Beijing, is originally from Singapore. He migrated to Australia and moved to Beijing six years ago. 'I originally wanted to work in Hong Kong but, because I speak Mandarin, they moved me to China.' Chieng initially worked for the China World Group, moving to Swissotel in 1993. Chieng, in charge of functions including balls, conferences and seminars, is an active hands-on manager who works hard to develop a positive attitude among his staff, and has created a quality-conscious team that enjoys good customer relationships.

Mr **Mark Gau**, an American-educated Taiwanese, has two jobs in China for the American multinational company, Sara Lee. He's director of new business development and also runs the sales and marketing function of a joint venture factory and retailing operation. While Sara Lee is best known for its luxurious and extravagant line of cakes and desserts, Gau is more concerned with the company's hosiery and socks division, broadly referred to as 'personal products'.

Gau arrived in October 1995 to live in Shanghai, having been involved in his company's China business since late 1992, initially from Singapore and then from Hong Kong. His family has lived in Taiwan for more than six generations; Gau moved to the United States in 1982 to study for his MBA before joining Sara Lee in 1991.

The joint venture business which takes up most of Gau's time manufactures pantihose, stockings and socks in a factory just outside Shanghai; a marketing and sales office is in the centre of town. The factory produces tens of millions of pairs of pantihose annually and employs around 1000 people.

Mr **Johnny Ho**, general manager of marketing for Foody's, a food and beverage manufacturing operation in Shanghai (a subsidiary of OOCL), is a Hong Kong Chinese who moved to China three years ago. Formerly heading up CPC, another food manufacturer, he was responsible for the manufacture and marketing of Knorr soups and condiments in China, a rapidly growing operation with several hundred staff. Foody's, his present organization, employs more than 300 staff in Shanghai in the manufacture of popular beverages. A full food and beverage business is planned. Ho takes a very sincere and open approach to managing local staff, focusing on training and empowering them. He's very popular, and gets good results.

Ms **Thu N. Ho**, Vietnamese by birth and American by nationality, has spent the last eight years managing a pharmaceuticals manufacturing operation in Shanghai's Minhang district.

Mr **Jim King** was born in China and educated in Taiwan, and then spent 15 years in the United States before returning, six years ago, to live in Beijing. Energetic and highly committed to his career in China, King is also a successful management trainer, coaching and teaching his own staff as well as contributing to high-profile public management training seminars. Having worked for Hewlett Packard in the US, he was posted to China for a Hewlett Packard joint venture on a three-year contract and, at the end of his tour, didn't want to leave. So he jumped ship to join Andersen Consulting, a systems integration consultancy associated with the well-known accounting firm, setting up their first office in China in collaboration with Tsinghua University. That done, he moved on to Novell Inc, the network software supplier, managing their Beijing operation and setting up a Shanghai office in 1996.

Mr **Lee Swee Chee** is a Malaysian Chinese who, for the last four years, has held the position of chief representative for computer and electrical industry giant, Honeywell, in Shanghai. He has achieved substantial progress in setting up his company's Shanghai operation and in creating an empowered team, the result of a sound hiring and training policy and an elaborate system of checks and balances. However, he describes it as an ongoing challenge. It is particularly demanding for someone almost constantly on business trips, as he is. Lee is active among the growing community of Malaysian Chinese living and working in Shanghai, helping to run the Malaysian Society.

Mr **Craig Pepples** is China country manager, based in Shanghai, for the Asian Sources Media Group, the largest trade publishing operation in Asia. Living and working in China since 1993, Pepples manages over 20 offices and more than 350 staff. With clients primarily drawn from the State-owned sector, ASM helps China-based exporters to penetrate Western markets, particularly in electronics, garments, gifts and household products.

A Chinese-language scholar from the United States, Pepples ('I admit I have "the China bug"') spent many years studying Chinese language and culture to the extent that 'I have it in my bloodstream'. He was influenced as a young man by elderly relatives who had been missionaries in Shanghai in its heydays during the 1920s and 1930s. Pepples takes a lively interest in the future prospects of the China market and particularly the evolution of a mainland Chinese business and management elite. With his long-term and deep knowledge of the State-owned sector and off-the-beaten-track parts of China, Pepples's experiences are in contrast with other China-watchers who are more interested in multinational companies in China.

Mr **Dan Shao**, a Chinese American, runs an entrepreneurial diversified trading and marketing operation in China, travelling back and forth between Los Angeles, Taipei and Shanghai up to six times a year. Over the last five years, he has spent up to 60 per cent of his time in China. Shao, originally born in Hong Kong of Shanghainese-speaking parents and so a Shanghainese speaker himself, migrated to Taiwan and then the United States, where he lived for 27 years. This biculturalism is definitely a plus for him on both sides of the Pacific.

Shao is particularly keen on developing his new hair and beauty products business, in which he promotes sales of imported, high-end products to salon professionals, training them in correct usage. His partner, Chinese Canadian Lynn Chen, holds classes in how to use cosmetics and accessories to improve personal image and style, using videos and individual demonstrations. Shao and his partner are planning to direct their sales increasingly towards consumers once they've established credibility and market awareness through the salon professionals.

Mr **Mark Thomas**, the manager of the Fitness Club at the Shanghai Hilton Hotel since mid-1994, has successfully built a team of local staff into a highly customer service-oriented group which now runs one of Shanghai's most popular fitness venues. His facility is run by 15 staff, serving daily around 150 members and hotel guests. Thomas, originally from the United Kingdom, previously worked in Hong Kong, where he also worked in a fitness club. Having backpacked around China, he acquired a taste for working there, and now speaks quite impressive Mandarin. He is a respected and popular member of Shanghai's expatriate scene.

Mr **Patrick Un**, a Singaporean based in China for nearly two years, was training manager for the US computer giant, Unisys; he now runs the Covey Leadership Center in Beijing. While with Unisys, Un was responsible for the training needs of over 200 staff across China; he trained PRC nationals to a level that met the requirements of a profit-driven and demanding multinational. After leaving Singapore, Un lived and worked in Australia and Germany for 11 years, and he brings an international, but still Chinese, view to his China assignment. Possessing a sense of humour, as well as a strong commitment to China, Un tries to put his experiences into perspective—to him, his assignment highlights the myths and realities of managing in China. Un advocates capitalizing on the opportunities offered in China today in order to develop yourself as well as others.

Mr **Michael Wu**, a Hong Kong Chinese who in 1992 crossed the border to live in mainland China, is general manager of the Holiday Inn, City Centre, Guangzhou, having been promoted from resident manager. Sophisticated and demanding, Wu is committed to improving quality throughout the hotel, in line with his experiences in the United States, Hong Kong and Singapore. Wu attended university in the US before joining

Acknowledgments

Shangri-La Hotels in Singapore and Hong Kong; he then spent three years in Canada. On his return to Asia, Wu considered that China offered the greatest opportunities—and challenges.

The author would also like to acknowledge the contribution made by the following people, who offered invaluable help and insights.

Simon Aliband of Quelle, Shanghai
Cristiana Barbatelli, formerly of Porta Asiatica, Shanghai
Oliver Barth of Jebsen's, Shanghai
John Beyer of China–Britain Trade Group, London
Lilian Bow of Colliers Jardine, Beijing
David Brock of Phoenix Pacific, Hong Kong
Jean Chan of Shanghai Sipra
Philip Chan of Synergy Consulting, Hong Kong
Alex Chang of Glaxo Wellcome, Beijing
C.K. Chang of Schmidt, Guangzhou
Tiffany Chang of Synergy Consulting, Beijing
John Chen of Ericsson, Taipei
Daniel Chieh of Schmidt, Shanghai
Peter Chou of Shine & Sagacity, Taipei
Ivy Chow of Norman Broadbent, Beijing
Eamonn Clarke of DHL, Beijing
John Dai of IBM, Beijing
James Deng of Ciba-Geigy, Beijing
Ding Yi, Edward, of Samsung, Beijing
Enrico Galderisi of Agip, Rome
Christine Greybe of Job Access, Hong Kong
William Hanbury-Tenison of Jardine Matheson, Shanghai
Stefaan van Hooydonk of China Europe International Business
    School, Shanghai
Nancy Huang, formerly of Swissotel, Beijing
Peter Kao of IBM, Taipei
Trish Kensell of Skill & Will, Shanghai
Andrew Key of the British Embassy, Beijing
Marsha King from Beijing
Tom King of Amrop, Hong Kong

Acknowledgments

Ken Kominski formerly of the Sheraton Hua Ting, Shanghai
David Kutena of Mannesmann Demag, Shanghai
Maurizio Lavezzini of Daedalus, Hong Kong
Catherine Lee of Creachine, Shanghai
Donna Lee of IBM, Taipei
Nandani Lynton of CCC Management Resources, Beijing
Henry Meng formerly of Amrop, Shanghai
Paul Moran, formerly of Siemens, Beijing
Anne Ng of Spencer Stuart, Shanghai
Anna Carin Nilsson of Ikea, Shanghai
Tom Pearce of Arco, Shekou
Nick Pennington formerly of Shell, Shanghai
Alison Pepples from Shanghai
Nathan Rosenberg of Phoenix Pacific, United States
Erik Rufer formerly of Sofitel, Shanghai
David Southworth of China Europe International Business
    School, Shanghai
Kathleen Speake of Mercer, Beijing
Ashley Steinhausen of Alliance, Shanghai
Jason Su of Shell, Shanghai
Dominic Tang of SEB Electric Appliances, Shanghai
James Tian of the Hilton Hotel, Beijing
Oskar Tondolo of Siemens Nixdorf, Beijing
Lela Tong of The Art of Business, Hong Kong
Johann Tse of John Swire & Sons (China), Beijing
Andy Tseng of DHL, Hong Kong
Linda Tremblay from the United States
Bob Vickers of DHL, Shanghai
Michel Vidal of the French Aviation Ministry, Beijing
Shane Walsh, formerly of International Nutrition Company,
    Shanghai
Simon Wan of Philips Lighting, Shanghai
Vincent Wan of Amrop, Hong Kong
Jeffrey Wang of Weicon, Shanghai
Wang Jing of Shell, Beijing
Ray Wang of I Will Not Complain, Beijing
Wang Shanping of Skill & Will, Shanghai

Acknowledgments

Stephen White of Interior Action, Shanghai
Irene Wolinski of General Motors, Beijing
Joerg Wuttke of BASF, Beijing
Ted Xia of Mettler Toledo, Shanghai
Cindy Yang of Shell, Shanghai
Leo Yang of Fuller, Shanghai
Jack Yeh of San Miguel, Beijing
Sophia Yeh of Shine & Sagacity, Taipei
Henry Yung of Horton, Shanghai
Sarah Zhao of EAC, Beijing

I would also like to express my thanks to Howard Ward and Nigel Campbell of the China Research Unit of the Manchester Business School in the United Kingdom for giving me permission to freely use the results of a survey they conducted in 1996. This material is of considerable significance and has been used extensively in the section on the expat experience in China.

There are many others who prefer to remain anonymous but to whom I nevertheless extend my thanks for their assistance.

Chronology

c.5000–4000 BC	Yellow Emperor, legendary progenitor of Chinese civilization
221–210 BC	Emperor Qin Shi Huang, founder of the Chinese Empire
618–907 AD	Tang Dynasty
907–960	Five Dynasties
960–1279	Sung Dynasty
1270–1368	Yuan Dynasty
1368–1644	Ming Dynasty
1644–1912	Qing Dynasty, including :
1662–1722	Emperor Kang Xi
1736–1799	Emperor Qian Long
1835–1908	Dowager Empress Ci Xi
1839–1842	Opium War
1850–1864	Taiping Rebellion
1893	Birth of Mao Zedong
1894–1895	Sino–Japanese War
1898–1901	Boxer Rebellion

Chronology

Introduction

In embarking on a career, or at least part of your career, in China, you must recognize why it is that you came here in the first place—was it for career advancement, to make money, to learn, to make a contribution? Be aware of the downside, which will include missing your friends, your home and your own culture. Above all, don't look back!

For many, China is for the 1990s what the Middle East was in the 1970s—foreigners go there to make money. You have a hard time, but you can save a bundle. This is one way of looking at it, but others have different views. Many expats find that China offers them the opportunity to make a bigger contribution than they could in their own countries; that they can have more autonomy away from head office; that they can cash in on the prosperity and fast-growth environment to make more rapid progress in their careers; that, if they are overseas Chinese, they can combine career advancement with 'returning to one's roots'; and that they can prove to themselves that they can adapt to an entirely different business environment with a quite different business culture.

Despite these attractions, all expats warn of problems, deprivations and hardships, and insist that a very high degree of commitment is needed to make a China posting successful, as well as the ability to maintain a balance in one's life. And remember, however long you are in China, however fluently you speak Chinese, however culturally attuned and sensitive you become, you will never really be Chinese, so you must keep in touch with your own cultural identity.

Making a contribution

As **Jim King** of Novell puts it, 'I wanted to stay in China beyond my first contract period, because I found the business environment to be so exciting, and I felt that what I was doing in the high technology field was what China wanted and needed. After six years in China, I really feel that I'm making a contribution, a much bigger contribution than I could make in the USA, where I spent 15 years, or in Taiwan, where I grew up. Also, working in China, which is so challenging and demanding, I have an opportunity to stretch myself and find out what I can do. I can find out how good I really am.'

The best opportunity for me

For **Johnny Ho**, China represents a great opportunity. 'Here I can make a difference. In China, I am better trained, speak better English, and have more experience than most other people. If I went to the USA or Europe, it would be much more competitive for me to get on, and I would not have the advantages. Here, I can make a big contribution helping to develop the local people. This is the main purpose of expats here.'

A chance for autonomy

Craig Pepples points out that multinational company executives working in China can get a free rein to grow something new. 'No-one in head office knew very much about China when I came here, so when I was asked to open a subsidiary in China, I was given a lot of autonomy. I was more or less left to run with it. China has lots of opportunities for the kind of person who likes freedom of action.'

'When water rises, the ship rises too'

For **Lee Swee Chee**, coming to China also meant great career opportunities. 'China is growing fast, so this is a great chance to move up,' he says. 'It's like the Chinese proverb, that when water rises, the ship rises, too. You can grow personally with these opportunities, you can be a pioneer, you can move faster up the corporate ladder than I could in Singapore, for example. You have a blank piece of paper. You can create an organizational culture. You can make history!'

But Lee warns of the long work hours, the exhausting travel schedule, and dealing with staff who '...often have an amazing lack of common sense' in a place where 'You can't take anything for granted, you have to cope with all kinds of delays and you have to check everything all the time. This is tiring. If things work out, it's a miracle! This is in great contrast with Singapore, where things tend to go smoothly most of the time. But, on balance, the advantages far outweigh the disadvantages, and the improvements in living conditions here over the last few years have been astounding.'

Time to return to the motherland

Patrick Un's view of China was originally influenced by opinions in his native Singapore. 'My family, originally from China, have been in Singapore for many generations, and it wasn't until I came to China that I realized how little I know about our original motherland,' Un says. It was not fashionable to speak Mandarin in Singapore schools in the 1970s, and many Singaporeans were educated entirely in English. 'People in Singapore at this time never thought they would have any reason to go to China,' Un reflects. 'Although for many Singaporeans, it's our original motherland, at that time China was thought of as old-fashioned, dirty, backward and full of people from the countryside. China had very negative connotations then.'

In 1979, Lee Kuan Yew introduced a national 'Speak Mandarin' campaign, but this took a long time to become fashionable. In the mid-1990s, however, things have changed. 'Judging by what I call barometers of trends—the behaviour of the yuppie class and television stars—Mandarin has gained wide acceptance in Singapore. Now, you can hear Mandarin being spoken in yuppie establishments and on TV programs,' Un says. It's taken more than a decade and a half, but now the view of China's official language is changing, and with it the view of China itself.

Other negative impressions of the PRC were held in Singapore, Un recalls. 'I heard of a business executive visiting China for the first time, and her main concern was that people in China spit in the streets. Spitting in public is one of those many things that are banned in Singapore.'

So when Un left Singapore for China, many fellow Singaporeans thought he was crazy. 'They are largely unwilling to sacrifice living in their clean, safe, efficient city to go abroad at all, let alone to China,' says Un, who made his decision on the strength of a friend's words, 'Our ancestors came from China; it is now time for us to return'. 'So when I came to China, I had all these images reflecting the beliefs of people in Singapore. But when I arrived, and found that some were true and some were not, all I could think was, "So what?"'

Another motherland returnee

Irene Wolinski, born in China of PRC Chinese parents who moved to Taiwan, also wanted to go back to the motherland—but as an expat, not as a local. 'When I told them I was going to work in China—I've been working in the USA for many years—my parents were most upset. "We worked hard to give you a good education, to send you to America, to give you a better life, to get you out of China, and what do you do? Go back to China!" they moaned. But all their efforts paid off, because I'm back here in China as an expatriate, with a good standard of living, but really back in my own environment, when I could never be completely at home in the USA.'

Distilling the best of East and West

For **Dan Shao**, who is running a business in China, success is not just wealth produced by his business. 'I ask myself this question all the time, "Why am I here and doing this business now in China?" With my background in China, Hong Kong and Taiwan, and having lived for so long in the US, I'm trying to distill the best of both the US and China and mix them together, and make my own contribution—and now's the best time.'

Making and joining a big family

Michael Wu's aims while working in China, especially in his hotel, are to create a family atmosphere, rather than just a working place, and thereby get the best out of the staff and feel that he's making a contribution. It's also part of his way of adapting to a very different business environment and management culture. 'In China, this is more necessary than anywhere else, and it's one thing I feel I'm doing here which works.' With this extra emphasis on being fair and caring, and providing a sense of belonging, Wu finds the challenge of working in China more demanding than in his previous working locations of Hong Kong and Singapore.

Make sure China is for you

Mark Gau has this advice for an executive coming to a China assignment. 'Think hard about why you are coming here: what is it doing to your family and your career; is the job satisfying career-wise and leading to career growth; how committed are you to China? You must use your common sense, make adjustments, and be culturally open and flexible but keep your values. You should have your family with you, if possible, otherwise you spend too much time with your staff and colleagues, and don't have much balance between work and leisure, especially because cultural and social activities in China can be limited.'

Maintain your own cultural identity

Simon Aliband considers that expats working in China should mix as much as possible with locals. 'Make the most of where you are now, appreciate your environment and surroundings, and see yourself as part of the society here. But be clear about your own cultural identity. Even if you can speak Chinese, if you're a foreigner, you will never be one of them. Always treat your experience here as an adventure, convince yourself that you are doing something special, that you are learning much more than you would at home. But always find something which is "normal" for you, to keep in touch with who you are.'

Remember the Golden Rules of China

1   Everything is possible.
2   Nothing is easy.
3   Western business logic does not apply.
4   It is a fun project if there is no deadline.
5   You must persist—things will come your way eventually.
6   Patience is the essence of success.
7   'You don't know China' means they disagree.
8   'New regulation' means they found a new way to avoid doing something.
9   'Internal regulation' means they are mad at you.
10   'Basically, no problem' means BIG problem.
11   When you are optimistic, think of Rule #2.
12   When you are discouraged, think of Rule #1.

Remember what non-PRC managers need for a successful China assignment

(An extract from a headhunter's specification, with thanks to Mr Henry Yung)

Technical competence.
Good leadership skills.
Cultural sensitivity.
Willingness to share and teach.
The ability to set a good example.
Consideration for others.
The sensitivity to avoid the subject of their salary or money issues.
The ability to place emphasis on purchasing power parity when income *is* discussed.

A good neighbour approach.
Respect for existing hierarchies and channels.
The ability to avoid losing one's temper.
The sensitivity to refuse to impose one's own personal values on local people.
Patience.
Modesty.
The realization of one's status as a guest in a host country.
The ability to be flexible on details yet firm on principles.
Taste and discretion.
Resourcefulness and adaptability.

Comments

Craig Pepples initially challenged the requirement to remember that 'you are a guest in this country'. 'There is an argument to say that you should treat everyone the same, and believe that you are the same. But probably, in the end, "You are a guest in this country" is good advice, as a way of coping with a dysfunctional environment, of surviving in your own bubble world.'

As **Lee Swee Chee** puts it, 'You must be a self-starter, independent, an action-oriented person, and be able to get things moving quickly. It may sound contradictory to now say this, but you have to be patient, too. You have to decide what you can and can't change. You have to be very aggressive in building market share for your operation, but you have to be patient with your staff. You need a split personality!'

Introduction

Author's notes

Throughout this book, the reader will notice personal names printed in bold type. These are the names of the main contributors to this book and are printed in bold type the first time they occur in each chapter. Information and biographical notes on the main contributors may be found in the Acknowledgments. People whose names are in ordinary type are described by reference to their company and location only.

The meaning of such terms as *laowei* are explained in the Glossary on pages 249–253.

The words 'Mandarin' and 'Chinese' are used interchangeably to refer to the standard form of the Chinese language spoken throughout China. Dialects such as Shanghainese and Cantonese are identified separately.

PART ONE

Managing in China: Concepts and Attitudes

Chapter 1

Your own personal approach

Most executives working in China, newly moved from a more Westernized or more mature business environment, will find a steeper learning curve than at any other time in their lives. Don't resist it, don't think that because you've negotiated business deals in Saudi Arabia or India that China will be easy. Prepare to assume that previous experience may not be relevant and adopt a learning mode. But don't see life as a battle for survival, as an ordeal to be coped with until you move on. Arguably, in a year in China, you can learn more about international business, about managing people and about managing yourself than in a decade anywhere else, because China is now transforming itself more rapidly than almost anywhere else on the planet.

Craig Pepples, who studied Chinese in the United States and lived in Hong Kong for several years before moving to China, felt that he had always tried to think about being in a 'learning organization'. 'I always regarded myself as being in learning mode, but I found that moving to China was a very intense learning process, so much so that I hardly had time to reflect on what I had learned! I think that most of the things I learned and am still learning have been and are now through helping others to learn, as the focus of so much of my work is training. This is true for most expatriates here today: it's our primary function.'

Michael Wu stresses the importance of keeping your learning up to date, and of the need to keep learning. 'Be sure to read as much as you can about the China situation as background information, and keep yourself informed about the people and social changes as well as political and economic changes. Because it's so difficult to obtain reliable information within China, you may find yourself asking friends in Hong Kong and elsewhere to keep clippings for you. But don't read anything written more than a year ago, or maybe even six months ago. It all changes too quickly.'

Life is an adventure

When you arrive in China, the odds are that everything will go wrong. Electrical appliances, such as kettles, irons and fax machines, will not respond when plugged in at your new apartment; at work, there is a shortage of telephone lines, the photocopying machine keeps breaking down, and staff members appear polite and friendly but are unable to understand or help you. Just get used to it quickly. Treat every new thing that goes wrong as one more step in the process of learning, coping and getting used to everything. When something unexpectedly works well, despite your caution and pessimism, feel relieved and pleasantly surprised!

Now, in early 1997, things everywhere are improving rapidly and Shanghai and Beijing in particular are quickly modernizing in all respects. Some China war stories now have a hint of the historical. But don't become complacent. As the *Beijing Scene Guidebook* points out, 'Those expatriates living in China on hardship packages may not want this news to leak out, but in comparison with the spartan days of the early 1980s, Beijing is no longer an exercise in deprivation. That said, it still ain't Kansas and the success of your China experience and overall mental well-being will hinge on your ability to reconcile the very different realities of your home country and your new home away from home.'

As part of the process of developing this ability, you will begin to get used to ambiguity, confusion and a lack of control. It often depends on where you've come from. The greater the familiarity and comfort of your previous location, the greater the unfamiliarity and discomfort of China. It can be easier and less of a shock to the system for a Westerner to come to China after a stay in Hong Kong or Taiwan, but it's still a shock. It also depends, of course, on the adaptability of your personality. As time goes on, these feelings of chaos and confusion will fade, but to a greater or lesser extent they will always be there, especially for non-Chinese speaking *gweilos* or *laowei*.

The important thing is to take a positive attitude, that this is all a big adventure, that this is definitely not boring, that those people who stay in Hong Kong or Singapore and run a China business from a safe and comfortable distance are just afraid of 'getting their hands dirty', of being 'in the war zone' and don't 'have the bottle' to actually *live* in China. Although, as pointed out above, the larger cities such as Shanghai and Beijing are a far cry from the hardships experienced when China first significantly opened up to foreign trade (and are also now in great contrast to the more remote cities, especially those in the interior), there is still a Marco Polo spirit, a pioneering attitude, among expats. Join them, share this! Get that feeling of camaraderie in adversity, of bonding. Meet and make friends with people, even from your own country, whom it would be impossible to meet and make friends with if you had stayed at home.

China is opening up more and more every day. History is being made every day. For example, those who took part in the first international rugby game in Shanghai for 50 years (the debut of the 'Shanghai Hairy Crabs'), those who played in the first formal cricket match in Shanghai for 50 years, and those who drank and made merry at the first British Chamber of Commerce Ball in Shanghai for 50 years—they know the feeling.

'On a personal level, for all of us living in China, it really is an adventure,' says Craig Pepples. 'It really is an honour and a heady thrill to be living in this environment of revolutionary change, where people around you are remaking themselves and their environments. For example, there are people I meet working in State-owned enterprises who are transforming their companies into competitive businesses—from loss-making dinosaurs into progressive, profitable operations. These changes are having an impact on everyone in the economy. There is so much turmoil, with people totally changing direction, and finding new energy in the process, and stress. But we must be prepared for the downside, the misunderstandings, and the disappointments and frustrations with the unrealization of expectations. Not everybody—neither the expatriate managers nor the people living here—can achieve their dream. China *is* an adventure, but one with risks.'

But actually living in China is certainly becoming less risky. **Alan Chieng** arrived in Beijing six years ago, when life was much more of an adventure than it is now. 'It was quite soon after the Tiananmen incident. There was a strict curfew at night. You were not allowed to be seen having local people as your friends. Lots of the expats had left. You had to carry your identity card around with you all the time. As soon as I arrived, I wanted to go home! But over the last six years, China has changed so much, and it's now much more comfortable.'

Learn to cope with the strange, the bizarre, the weird
Every day, you'll be reminded of the alienness of being a non-PRC person working in China, especially if you're a Westerner—although you can take comfort from the fact that it is nothing like as alien as it once was. Even executives who speak Mandarin have never been to a place where the people have such an alien mind-set.

A Western sales executive originally from the United States, who speaks Mandarin well after many years in

Taiwan, commented, 'I speak Japanese and I'm married to a Japanese, but I think China, where I've also spent many years, is much more bizarre than Japan. I think it's because of its history. The experience of the Cultural Revolution and the Communist political system, which is half-breaking down, especially economically, together with the oriental heritage which is in itself perplexing to Western-ers, gives foreigners a double whammy of weirdness when they come to China. Japan has the oriental strangeness but doesn't have the strange Communist system. China is the strangest place on earth!'

Knowing that other people share your feelings—even people for whom China should be less, rather than more, weird—will help you cope more confidently, and every day China is becoming more Westernized, especially in the large cities.

'Sometimes I even feel nostalgic for how weird China was four or five years ago,' says Craig Pepples. 'You still see people walking down the streets carrying birds in cages, wearing pyjamas all day in public and hanging washing in the trees, but you don't see the Mao suits very often any more. People now wear Western clothes in a Western way. They don't leave the labels on the outside of the suit sleeves any more, and they wear proper shoes with their suit, not training shoes! And you don't see the Nescafe jars with a few tea leaves floating around inside like you used to. You're probably more likely to see them clutching a can of Coke.'

Pepples has also noticed that some of the stranger aspects of customer service in China have now changed. 'There was a time when I was on board an aircraft in China and I asked for a refill of my coffee. The stewardess simply said "No!". You don't come across this so often any more. China has now woken up to more Western-style customer service.'

Mark Thomas also reflects on how Shanghai has lost much of its raw, pioneering spirit, compared with even two years ago. Talking about the situation when he first came to Shanghai, Thomas says, 'The electricity was often off at night, and there were relatively few bars and places to go. In 1990, life was even more basic, there were fewer expats, it wasn't easy to put together a team to play rugby or other sports. Now there's a wealth of choice.'

Take each day as it comes

Don't have inflexible expectations about the results you can achieve by specific dates, about your lifestyle or anything about your new world in China. Take each day as it comes. As Irene Wolinski of General Motors in Beijing puts it, 'I used to have firm goals for every project completion, for every plan I was working on, as I did in the USA. But it just didn't work here. I just got more and more frustrated and felt under more and more pressure, but I couldn't do anything. So I gave up having such fixed objectives. I still make goals, but I tend to keep things much more fluid. It's impossible to know what will happen from one day to the next, and you have to keep yourself open for new possibilities.'

Because it's difficult to plan your tasks, because the unexpected crops up constantly, and because the demands of staff unfamiliar with their duties can be almost incessant,

19

many executives find it impossible to get through their daily jobs and tend to find themselves working overtime in the evenings and at weekends as a matter of routine.

'This can seem onerous and tough, and can heighten the feeling of sacrifice you're making if you've just moved from a more predictable business environment, where you had time to see your friends and relax at evenings and weekends,' reflects one Western expat who has moved to Shanghai from Hong Kong. 'But the good news is that it gets easier. After a few months down the track, you find you manage to get the work done. The local staff still keep asking questions—often unbelievable, like "Where shall I go for lunch?" and "Do I have to come at the same time tomorrow?", but they become more and more resourceful and do develop initiative.

'After a few months, I was able to put my head above water and discover that there was a life outside the office. But it's still impossible to reserve more than 40–50 per cent of each day for your own jobs. You must allow a lot of time to deal with the unexpected. If you ever find that you have time on your hands, it's a moment of real wonder!'

Learn to handle culture shock
As explained by Dr Nandani Lynton in the *Beijing Scene Guidebook*, 'Foreigners [and to a certain extent overseas Chinese] moving to live and work in a new country commonly experience a period of transition entailing some degree of anxiety, confusion and disruption...daily signals and rituals one relies on suddenly disappear or are replaced by new and unknown signals. Everything is new—the language, forms of socialising, food, business

practices and hours. The reaction is an emotional roller-coaster...

'Despite individual differences, culture shock tends to accord with the following progressive stages: The Honeymoon; The Crisis; Rejection; Adoption and Adjustment.' During the Honeymoon stage, '...the newly relocated person is excited about his/her surroundings. Everything is interesting, quaint and exciting...from arrival to about six weeks later, until you hit the Crisis. The excitement has worn off, the difficulties are apparent, the stress is felt. What was quaint only last week is now seen as dirty. Things go wrong...' The Crisis usually continues into week twelve and bottoms out into Rejection.

During Rejection, 'All the frustration and anger collected during the Crisis stage gets blamed on...the local culture...the waitress who brings the wrong dish, the traffic jam, the electricity black-out...home looks wonderful in comparison... foreigners seek places filled with their own countrymen...some never go beyond this stage, others leave the country. Those who stay on and work to overcome their culture shock enter Adaptation and Adjustment.'

Then, 'The rosy Honeymoon view and the black Rejection view combine into a realistic picture of the new culture. Foreigners start to feel at home in their new surroundings; they feel comfortable getting around, and they begin to develop a social network. Six months after arrival, 10 per cent are feeling on top of things, 50 per cent feel comfortable, 35 per cent are getting along, and 5 per cent are still in Rejection.'

Strategies for overcoming culture shock include having 'a sense of humour, the ability to let go of fixed ideas, a healthy curiosity, and learning enough of the language to get around by oneself; also, developing an interest in local culture and, above all, creating a social network.

'Especially if the group includes people from different cultures, it can be an invaluable source of support and shared experience. On those days when a lonely expat wonders what he or she is doing so far from home, relationships with people who are at home right here can be solace enough.'

Management styles in China

As **Jim King** explains, 'You must be prepared to be adaptable in your management style to succeed in China.' Echoing Irene Wolinski's words, King maintains that 'You must have patience with what you can achieve, especially at first. The environment is often difficult, and you have to live with being less productive, especially to cope with all the bureaucracy. You just can't expect to get things done at the same rate that you would do in the USA, for example.'

Patrick Un's management style has also changed. As a result of a wider scope of responsibilities and having to be more hands-on and proactive than is normally required in his native Singapore, 'I've become a lot more patient, persistent and versatile; more goal oriented and opportunity driven. It's all part of the bigger challenge which working in China represents.'

Those executives used to working on their own, used to leaving their staff unsupervised for long periods, used to expecting their staff to work largely on their own initiative and be able to solve problems on their own, will experience deep culture shock. Things simply won't get done. You just have to be much more hands-on.

'Staff in China, especially those who have worked in the State sector, will expect to be told in detail everything they have to do,' says one Western executive who works in the service sector between Shanghai and Beijing. 'If the slightest variation in the expected situation occurs, they will immediately, without thinking, ask what they should do. Responsibility and decision-making are, for them, to be avoided at all costs. They don't think about the rewards of doing a good job; they contemplate, with horror, the possible punishments they may suffer for making a mistake. So, you just can't operate with a management style that focuses on delegation and individual autonomy, at least not for some time. It can take several months of training, coaching and support-giving to promote a sense of responsibility and initiative.'

Some Western executives worry about returning to their home countries with their new China-influenced management approach. 'I think staff in the UK would feel that I was being patronising, interfering, rule-obsessed, bossy and even insulting to them if I went back to the UK and treated them as I do my staff in China,' one British expat reflected, looking somewhat shocked at the idea. 'I tend to treat my staff in China like we're all members of a family, and I'm mother, or big sister, or whatever. This seems to work here. But imagine doing this in Britain! I don't think I would last five minutes!'

Mark Thomas, based in Shanghai, sees a gradual transition away from an authoritarian management style towards more democratic and consensus-oriented management methods in China, especially in view of the expanded economy and the increased mobility of local staff. 'It's impossible to be very tough these days, because staff will just leave,' he comments. 'A manager in one of the foreign hotels in Shanghai who insisted that his staff bow to him every morning just wasn't allowed to get away with it.' Thomas also mentioned an incident where an expatriate friend was forced to resign after losing his temper and physically attacking a local supervisor.

Be a leader—China style

Jim King says that if you're not a PRC local and you're running a business in China, '...you must show a very strong commitment to being in China to be accepted by your staff. In fact, I would say you must have a passion for China.' Such a Sinophile quality is vital in the land of the Middle Kingdom, where generations of Chinese have been brought up to believe in their inherent and unquestionable superiority over all other nations on earth. 'Other countries are also known for latent chauvinism, but in China, it's something of an art form,' commented one Western expat executive.

Leading a group of Chinese staff must therefore include an acknowledgement of this well-understood fact in order to meet their expectations and make them feel more comfortable. You must certainly acknowledge that, even if it was not always the case, since the early 1980s, China's century has come. The rising generation in China's major cities know this only too well: their parents had a hard time, they've been told repeatedly—they're the lucky ones.

Mark Gau shares this strong sense of mission, of wanting to help China to improve and develop as part of his contribution to being here. 'It's very important to show this to your staff and to your Chinese partner. They have to feel that you have this sentiment and this sense of commitment. Present yourself positively; as their leader, this makes them more positive.'

> *You reap what you sow.*
> *How one treats others is like seeing one's own face in a mirror.*
> *If you smile, you see a smiling image.*
> *If you frown, a frowning image stares back at you.*

CAI GEN TAI *(Roots of Wisdom)* c. 1630

Leadership in China has specific connotations. China's leaders are traditionally strong, autocratic, even ruthless. The most successful emperors, before and after the Qing dynasty, have been described as such. In management, these qualities must be tempered with team-building, motivation of staff, and an emphasis on empowerment and developing initiative. However, don't draw attention to any perceived weaknesses and indecisiveness if one wishes to gain the respect of one's local staff.

Lee Swee Chee says, 'You need a strong leadership style to build a team in China. If managers are too nice, they don't get respect. Look at the most successful leaders in the history of China—they were all tough. Some of the most outstanding emperors, and the Great Helmsman himself, were extremely tough. You must have an iron fist. You must be prepared to run a kind of benevolent dictatorship, to take a no-nonsense attitude.'

Johnny Ho adds, 'Although you must be a strong leader, don't treat the local people as inferior, especially if you're an overseas Chinese. The only difference between you and them is that you were more lucky, your parents took you away from China; so try to mix with the local people socially, but don't trust them too soon. And I tell the young expat guys not to fall in love with local girls—they may just want you for your foreign status and money. You should use the opportunity of working in China to save money, which you can do easily here. In contrast, Hong Kong and Taiwan are so expensive.

'You should treat local people very sincerely and take an interest in their careers, especially in Shanghai. They are born business people and will soon move up. As a leader in China, your job is to train them and encourage them.'

Mark Thomas feels that his staff keep looking to him for instructions, '...but I would rather they thought for themselves more, and shared their problems with me'. The way to achieve this, Thomas has found, is to build informal, private relationships ('They don't want to speak up in a group meeting') and get to know the supervisors well ('The supervisors would tell me if someone's going to leave before they do').

Thomas has been able to develop leadership abilities in his team by introducing some specific job demarcations. His staff were all generally referred to as 'Health Club attendants' when he arrived, which tended to discourage individuals taking responsibility and displaying any leadership qualities. Staff were given no encouragement to grow and they avoided attempts at empowerment. So he started to give them highly specific jobs in different parts of the club. 'Now it's possible to blame someone if a job is not done. Now, if there's no toilet paper in the ladies' toilet, or no water in the drinking dispenser in the gym, I know who's to blame. We're talking about introducing some incentive schemes, like the way it's done in Hong Kong. Already, the masseuses get a percentage on the number of customers, and I'm hiring other specialized people, like a swimming instructor and a tennis coach.'

Craig Pepples observes that people in China expect leaders to conduct themselves like emperors, divinities, beings who are out of touch with the common people and who are not concerned with small details. 'When I went on a tour of Beijing and Tianjin with our CEO, we were greeted with extreme politeness,' Pepples recalls. 'We were treated with incredible courtesy, and the arrangements were highly ceremonial, designed to shield us from the mundane and everyday things. But this cannot be sustained. Every day my staff see me in my office in Shanghai, warts and all. So I just can't be an emperor. I think that all expat bosses, in the eyes of their staff, undergo a demystification stage, a kind of "Emperor's New Clothes" syndrome, when the local people gradually realize you're just human.'

Pepples's leadership style is team-oriented and encourages self-learning. 'This is tough, but once our staff appreciate this, then they stay with us because of it.' Every company, Pepples maintains, goes through 'the Emperor stuff' phase, basically because they are forced into it by the staff. 'The staff have a predisposition to being ruled by an emperor, but you can change this, you can create a different culture. We've tried to create a culture of team-work, and even though this was initially at odds with the expectations of the local staff, it has actually become a reality and now an attraction.'

Pepples also insists that to be an effective leader you need to show personal commitment, and care for each individual staff member. 'You must build human relationships here. This has enormous value. That's why people talk about *guanxi* all the time; *mei guanxi* means "it doesn't matter". If your relationships with people on your staff and others breaks down, you will not be effective as a leader. You will make no progress.'

Philip Chan, who runs an insurance business in Shenzhen, points to another very important quality and requirement for a successful leader in China—living in China. 'You won't get any respect from the China people unless you live in China,' he says. 'You have to live with them, and see the China market through their eyes. Otherwise you can make big mistakes and make quite wrong assumptions. For example, I used to think that Shenzhen people, because they're in Guangdong province, would speak Cantonese! Of course they don't, because many of them have relocated from the north of China. And it wasn't until I learned to speak Mandarin myself [Chan is a Hong Kong Chinese] that I was really respected by them.'

Alan Chieng finds that his staff like him to be their leader, to the extent that they don't want to take any instructions from their immediate supervisors. 'People want to do a job to increase the power and importance of their boss so that in turn they are made to appear more important. They can't get this if they do a job for a supervisor who's also fairly junior, even though he reports to this higher boss. I try to establish a hierarchy so that I don't have too many direct reports, so I delegate to the banquet service manager who delegates to the captain who delegates to the waiters. But the captain likes to come directly to me for instructions. Being a leader in China means that everyone wants to report directly to you—but you can't run a large operation this way! So you have to build up the importance of their supervisors in their eyes.'

Being a leader in China can be very different from being a leader anywhere else. For over a year, Nick Pennington was head of the East China region for Shell, the major oil company, based in Shanghai. 'In Shell, we had our own ideas of what constituted leadership. Much of this was bound up in the fact that Shell was a very old-established, large and global company, and wherever you went people respected you and looked up to you as a leader. When I came to China, I met people who had never heard of Shell! They just saw me as a funny-looking *gweilo* with red hair, working for some foreign company. It was very sobering. I had to rethink my whole attitude to the definition of leadership qualities and how I should behave as a leader. My whole context was suddenly missing.'

Michael Wu emphasizes that leadership in China must be very up-front and obvious. 'You must show your staff that you're a good leader, that you are hard-working, and that you care about the business, and about them. You must make a genuine effort to win their respect.' Wu combines this with a strategy of creating a sense of belonging in the hotel, of providing a family atmosphere, not just a place to work.

This father-figure, family-oriented aspect of running a business in China should not be underestimated. One expat woman executive, working in Shanghai, makes these observations: 'When I came to work in China, it was my first job with managerial responsibilities, my first opportunity to be a leader. I kept thinking that if I'd had management experience in a more "normal" environment, it may have been easier. But, more importantly, it would have been more useful if I'd had experience as a mother! I've found that one of the best leadership techniques is to create a feeling of family. So I copied my own mother, combining strictness and laying down rules with caring and fairness, and of being quite clear about when they've done well and when they've made mistakes. Sometimes I think I can't do it, treating my staff as if they are kids! But it does seem to work in this context, at this point in time.'

Exercising successful leadership in China, as in many other contexts, includes gaining the respect of your staff—in China, however, it can be a slower process than anywhere else. Because China was for so long closed to the outside world, many expats find that there's a large measure of suspicion. It can take a considerable time for staff to feel comfortable but when they do, this respect can last and last. When respect is lost, however, it's almost impossible to retrieve. Being a leader in China means showing that you know what you're doing, that you're the expert and the arbiter; if you fail to live up to these expectations, you may have lost your 'Mandate from Heaven'. It is well to bear in mind the fate of the wife in this Chinese proverb, which makes the point that it is as difficult to win back love as it is to retrieve spilt water:

> *A prince of the Zhou dynasty was, as a humble young man without titles, so devoted to learning and so uninterested in earning a living, that his wife divorced him. When his talents as a scholar, administrator and soldier were discovered by the King and he was given the title of Prince of Qi, his wife pleaded for a reunion. But he took a bowl of water and threw it to the ground, and asked her to retrieve it. But all she could gather was mud.*

'Spilt water cannot be retrieved' (Chinese proverb, Shi Yi Ji)

Be firm yet flexible

Principles are values, long-term goals and deeply-held beliefs, such as honesty, integrity, a commitment to being in China to give and to take, caring about others, and being equally fair to all staff, customers and suppliers according to a basically meritocratic system. These must be stated and then not changed; actual implementation should basically support the principles but need not be so inflexible. Therefore you need to be firm on principles and flexible on details.

These comments by one expat executive illustrate these statements. 'You may have a principle that staff pay is reviewed at regular times, say every half-year, but you could still pay bonuses in the meantime. And you may have specific vacation timings and guidelines, but if a staff member's family member is sick and they're a long way from home, you should be flexible in making exceptions. But you have to make clear that it's an exception, that it shouldn't happen often, and that it does not become a standard.'

Customers in China are always asking for discounts (something that will be discussed in more detail later). While you may have very specific rules about the kinds of discounts that are allowed, showing some flexibility can make customers feel special. Any such flexibility should, however, support your basic principles, not conflict with them. They should involve finding a way to make the customers feel that they're getting a great deal, while keeping your basic discounting guidelines intact.

Learn to handle a heavy work-load
There will be many occasions when your working hours are long, obstacles occur that make your job difficult, you get frustrated, and you find yourself having to do jobs that others should have done. Patrick Un found long working hours were the least of his problems. 'I spent my first few months in China keeping a cool head, keeping healthy and learning the system, especially having to get used to the lack of Singapore-style conveniences. For example, in Singapore, hospitals try to schedule their hours to suit the convenience of customers. Not so in China. I had to queue up at 3 am one winter morning, with the temperature at minus five degrees celsius, to make sure I got an appointment for a sick friend. People in Singapore just don't realize how fortunate they are, with telephone banking, telephone reservations, all kinds of information sources, and even airport transit shopping!'

During his first month, Un worked all 30 days and all the weekends, setting up his department, and the pace has continued. Why was this necessary? 'I spend a lot of time on admin stuff, such as organising visas, obtaining basic information, organising repairs, overcoming telecommunications breakdowns. These aren't really part of my job but they must be done in order for my real job to get done.'

Michael Wu found that despite his promotion to General Manager of his hotel, his working hours were still unusually long. 'I looked forward to having a job as GM, after working as resident manager and in other positions. In Hong Kong and Singapore, GMs are seldom seen after 6 pm or 7 pm. But here I'm still working until late in the evening trying to empower people, encouraging them to care, to help guests when things go wrong, and training them to use their initiative more.

'I must persevere with the staff to achieve the results I want. I still worry, after four years, that the staff are taking it easy the moment I return to my apartment at night. Visible management is very important in China. You have to be seen to be walking around keeping an eye on things. So I work much longer hours than if I was working outside of the PRC.'

Perseverance
A rope pulled back and forth will eventually cut through wood.
Water falling drop by drop will eventually wear through stone.
The melon will eventually ripen and fall from the vine.

CAI GEN TAI *(Roots of Wisdom)* c. 1630

Mark Thomas says, 'Expatriates in the Hilton in Shanghai are expected to work at least 12 hours a day, with just one day off a week. When I worked in Australia, it was eight hours a day with two-day weekends, and even in Hong Kong, although we worked 10 hours a day, we always got two days off a week. In China, the working hours are really the demands of your management responsibilities, not so much the function of the job itself. Hilton watches all the expats carefully and it would be noted and commented upon if you were late.'

At Swissotel in Beijing, the GM, a German, was so fed up with asking staff to paint a door and finding nothing happened, that he ordered a tin of paint and a brush with the intention of doing the painting job himself. He didn't have to do it himself because the staff were then so embarrassed they immediately started work. This story is not unusual—and such tactics usually work!

The importance of knowing the language

The world seems a much less perplexing, confusing and hostile place once you start speaking some Chinese. Many *laowei* are put off by the massive effort and huge investment of time and effort required to be fluent in the language. Indeed, those foreigners with great confidence and fluency in the language spent several years of study at a relatively young age to get to that stage.

For non-Chinese, learn some Putonghua
Although linguistic ability is an immeasurably huge advantage, even a smattering of simple greetings is unquestionably better than nothing. Some foreign executives who feel 'I'm in China to run a business, not to go back to school! I don't have time for all this back-to-school stuff' are doing themselves a disservice. Just a few hours of effort can

bring a smile to the faces of local ministry officials, customers, suppliers and other important contacts, and (probably most importantly) show your staff your commitment to being in China—as well as affording them frequent opportunities for amusement.

Even a partial understanding of the language can lead to a quantum leap in an understanding of the Chinese mindset. Quite simply, if there is no equivalent in Chinese of an English concept, then people would not think about it. How could they, when the words do not exist? For Patrick Un, although he primarily trains in Mandarin, the English language is used for management concepts such as presentation skills, facilitating, mentoring, empowerment and the like. For non-Chinese executives working in China, understanding why these concepts do not translate well is part of the process of understanding Chinese thinking, and can help dramatically in working with a local staff.

If you ask a non-Chinese PRC-based executive if they have any regrets on leaving China, the odds are that they will say that they wish they'd learned more, or even some, Chinese. Don't be one of them!

Mark Thomas's attempts to learn Chinese (which have been reasonably successful) are mainly to show his commitment to China and to build relationships with the local people. 'Actually,' he says, 'it's more important that my staff improve their English than I improve my Chinese, but for me it's meant that I'm not insulated from the local scene, and I'm able to visit local places. I see too many foreigners treating lack of English language ability in the locals as a sign of stupidity. I remember one Western expat in the hotel complaining about one of his staff members because his English was still poor after two years in the hotel. The staff member turned to him and said politely, "But you have been in China for five years and you can't speak one word of Chinese!"'

For most foreigners, learning Chinese, especially how to read and write it, takes a huge amount of perseverance and persistence. But those who have achieved it put to shame those who give up. When struggling with this seemingly insurmountable task, it is inspiring to remember the story of Li Bai and the old woman who was grinding a rod into a needle:

> *A young man, named Li Bai, decided to give up his studies when he felt that his progress in learning was poor. As he walked home from his university, having abandoned his work, he saw an old woman who was laboriously working at grinding down a large iron rod. When Li Bai asked her what she was doing, she replied curtly, 'Making a needle of it'. Then, feeling ashamed of his own lack of perseverance, Li Bai decided to return to his studies. Subsequently, he was recognized as a great scholar and one of the leading poets of the Tang Dynasty.*

'Grinding a rod into a needle' (Chinese proverb, Qian Que Lei Shu)

For overseas Chinese, learn some local dialects
Overseas Chinese—from Taiwan, Hong Kong, Singapore and elsewhere—can find themselves feeling like *laowei* in places like Shanghai, where the local dialect is favoured above Mandarin. If Shanghainese people see a Chinese face, they will speak Shanghainese. They're proud and patriotic about their city, and this is one of their ways of showing it. If you can reply in Shanghainese, it is a good way to win a friend, or at least avoid being overcharged!

Many overseas Chinese working in China have distant relatives still living in China, and may remember some of their dialects from their parents and other relatives. This is an undoubted advantage. Knowing a local dialect also demonstrates that you are making a commitment to a career in China.

As **Dan Shao** explains, 'Being able to speak Shanghainese is a huge advantage. Not only in avoiding being ripped off by taxi drivers and getting what I want shopping, but in business negotiations. First of all, my potential local partners think of me as a foreigner, even though I'm speaking Mandarin. At best, I'm seen as an overseas Chinese. But when I start speaking Shanghai dialect to them, their attitude changes completely. I'm like their long-lost brother. It's amazing! I feel very lucky in this way. But it is possible to learn a few words of Shanghainese and use these to great effect. It gives a lot of "face" to Shanghai people. This would be well worth the effort.'

Learning Cantonese has now become very fashionable among PRC nationals from central and northern China who have come to live in the south. It's seen as sophisticated (mainly because of Hong Kong) and also goes a long way in doing business in Canton and Guangdong province. Many overseas Chinese, such as those from Malaysia, already speak Cantonese having spoken it during childhood. Other overseas Chinese can reap great benefits by catching up with them, although it's seen as challenging and fraught with *faux pas*. But these can all add to the entertainment!

Working with the political system

It is important that the expatriate manager in China understands that you may have to manage too many, rather than too few, staff, and that you may have to live with the situation. One Western car dealership in Shanghai found itself having to employ the brother of a senior party official in order to please its Chinese partner. The company tried to make the best of the situation, and found their new uninvited staff member to be really quite good. And, naturally, possessed of excellent *guanxi*!

It's not always possible to make such a virtue out of a necessity, however. Anyone visiting a restaurant in China, joint venture or not, will be amazed at the excessive number of staff—and the huge underemployment this represents. This situation is a reflection of the political system and tends to lead to more job demarcation, a further unwillingness to take responsibility, more gossiping and the formation of cliques.

What can be done about this? Mark Thomas is one expat who feels that on the whole he has too many staff, but they are subject to the manning levels laid down by the hotel and can't easily be changed. 'When we're very busy, we need all these staff, but when it's quiet, these people often don't have much to do. So they spend a lot of time gossiping. How do you manage people who are underemployed? There's a limit to the number of times they can keep cleaning out the toilets. So I encourage them to help the members and guests to use the equipment correctly, and chat to them, not just among themselves.' Thomas's club now has the reputation of being one of the friendliest in Shanghai.

However, Thomas warns that overstaffing is, to a certain extent, required in a China operation. 'You can't assume that you can get the same performance from your staff in China that you would get from a Hong Kong or a UK team. It takes time to build up productivity.'

Ensure you maintain the 'face' of an existing boss
It is not politically astute to undermine the authority of existing supervisors and managers when you take over a joint venture. You are there to represent the foreign partner, while the management should be a shared task. The best advice is to build relationships with the established managers, seek their advice and get them on your side. If you cause them to lose face, they can exercise retribution. If you give them face, they can help you. If they resist any necessary changes you may have to make, encourage them to see the reasons for these changes.

Work with the unions
In a manufacturing operation in Shanghai (as in many other joint ventures in China), a number of the staff are Party members and insist on attending union meetings, organized by the Chinese partner. All staff are obliged to go, so it is necessary for the expat manager to understand labour union requirements and work within them, minimizing, as far as possible, loss of earnings. Foreign senior management has found, however, that in the clash between political consciousness and commercial viability, often the latter wins, especially if it means bonuses for the Government and the Chinese partner. A foreign manager

says, 'If there's a crisis in production and I can't afford to let a whole shift of people go to the union meeting, then I can ask them not to go and they'll stay at work.'

Respect the Chinese authorities
It will make your life easier if you understand that the need for 'social control' is a top priority for the Chinese authorities: part of their role is to in censor information-related materials, control all media and implement other 'social control' activities. Westerners and overseas Chinese enjoy receiving foreign newspapers and magazines while living in China, especially when they can read stories about China. Many expats lament the lack of news and, in particular, information on what is going on around them. Unfortunately, the *China Daily* has relatively few admirers among the expat population due to its formal style and scant detail on anything interesting, although locals learning English have been known to enjoy it, and its standards of written English are passable.

However, having finished reading your precious copy of the *Far Eastern Economic Review* or *The Economist*, it's not a good idea to pass them on to your local staff to read. To them, it's a foreign view of China, it's bound to be 'wrong', and it would not do for them to learn about these 'wrong' ideas—it may get them into trouble. Better not to read it.

Chinese authorities tend to get very worried about big crowds of people, for whatever reason they have formed. Although large crowds tend to be orderly and are no problem, it is wise to respect the anxiety of the *gong an* and other law enforcement agencies and keep a low profile. In any encounter with the authorities, be extremely polite and respectful. The local people are very frightened of them, so they're used to instant obedience from everyone, which includes foreigners and overseas Chinese.

Dealing with infrastructure problems

You need to understand the limitations of what can, and cannot, be achieved in your working environment. Craig Pepples says, 'You'll get a nervous breakdown if you expect to be able to work at the same pace in China as you would in Hong Kong or other mature office environments. When you're working in a fairly advanced economy, you just think about what you're doing, and all the work gets done. You don't think about all the logistics. But here, you have to think about all the basics. The telephones, the electric power, the copying machines, transport, deliveries. It's like going back from advanced computing to the days of binary codes. Even the most fancy, expensive buildings in Shanghai and Beijing are not without infrastructure problems. You can never be entirely free of simple mechanical breakdowns and the problems that result; they can completely disrupt your work.'

In the summer of 1996, Shanghai faced hotter-than-average weather conditions at a time when many new office buildings and new apartment blocks were being built and occupied. Power consumption rose to over seven million kilowatts at peak demand, when Shanghai city's power capacity was only five million, and power had to be pumped in from surrounding Zhejiang province. Ironically, just as the *Shanghai Star* English-language weekly reported, 'There will not be any requirement to impose power usage restrictions', offices in the downtown Huahai Road Central were invaded by uniformed officials demanding air-conditioning be shut down for two days, with a penalty of RMB 10,000 for non-compliance. No office, no matter how expensive and upmarket, could avoid this directive, unless they had their own generators.

Get the resources you need
If you are managing a team within a bigger office, or in any situation where you have to share resources, the amount of recognition you get as an effective leader will be in direct proportion to how good you are at getting new telephone lines, getting someone in to mend the fax and copying machines, and getting a new computer for your staff: resources are power. However, in order to get what you and your staff need, you may have to get tough and this may lead to a deterioration in relationships with others in the office, including other expat managers fighting for resources for their staff. This can't be helped—you must be seen as capable of getting things moving, and be seen to care. In some ways, expats have an advantage here, because often the providers of these resources and the delivery and mending thereof don't want to lose face with the foreigners or overseas Chinese.

Work in good conditions
When looking at office accommodation, you have to strike a balance between an expensive yet 'status-conferring' smart address and the cost savings you may be able to achieve by moving into premises reminiscent of a State-owned enterprise.

Chinese staff assume that all multinational companies have smart offices in the most expensive hotels in town, or in gleaming new office towers. This is largely true, but many of the multinationals are finding these unbelievably expensive, and actually threatening the viability of their China operations. But to move into a very substandard office—which in China can mean mice, cockroaches, power breakdowns, draughts, damp, and appallingly neglected buildings—is not the answer. Better to find a cheaper location but keep up the internal office standards. Living and working conditions are important for motivation and productivity, to say nothing of the impression given to customers.

Maintain your office standards

Once you've established a good multinational office environment, don't let it degenerate. Lee Swee Chee considers it very important to set a high standard to start with in terms of your office environment and office routine, and then keep checking everything. 'The staff must be shown how things should be done,' he explains. 'Then there should be regular follow-up to make sure the standards are maintained.' Lee admits to a Singaporean attitude towards cleanliness as part of his insistence on high quality. 'I'm not saying that I will fine everyone $150 if they don't flush the toilet, but I want them to take a pride in things being tidy and clean, as a requisite for high-quality work.'

Lee regularly walks around the office to check on office discipline, tidiness and the general level of activity. 'There used to be papers all over the floor, and sometimes the carpets were dirty and people did not look presentable,' he says. 'But now, because people know I will tell them off and then they will be embarrassed, they're much tidier. They believe in the importance of presenting a high-quality image in the office, including in their personal appearance. I don't have to walk around the office quite so much now. The percentage of my time which I have to spend on people problems is now much diminished, but it has taken me at least three years to reach this situation. I still walk the office on a regular basis with my office manager, stopping to look at anything which is a mess.'

Put phones high on the agenda

Telecommunications and their presence or lack thereof are a good indicator of the extent of a country's economic development. A lack of telephone lines is less and less of a problem in the PRC, but the density is still much less than in developed countries. In most offices, staff share telephone lines, sometimes to an extent where productivity is affected, and getting through on the telephone is rarely easy in any but the largest multinational offices. Here a mobile can certainly help, and it also makes a big difference when stuck in traffic, as it enables an executive to more or less carry on working. It can also be helpful in getting through to the main office when all the numbers are busy.

It can be a practical gesture for an expat to share his or her mobile with the most senior local staff, with strict instructions for careful usage. Some expats leave their mobiles with their local staff in the evenings and at weekends to deal with customers who call (who are rarely mindful of the day or time of day when they need something). Expats unable to speak Chinese will always find a mobile a great way of getting out of trouble. If you get lost in a taxi, simply call the person you're on your way to visit and ask them to get a member of their local staff to speak to the taxi driver.

Mobile phones are also undeniably symbols of power and prestige (the Chinese slang word for mobile telephone means 'Big Brother'—the kind running a secret society) and their use should be limited to only the most senior people in a company (bearing in mind their purchasing and running expenses). But you may find that you don't need to buy mobiles for your staff: they may have them already, and many more have pagers. However, this can be a sign of moonlighting activities on the side, of which you may or may not approve.

Learn how your staff live

You will probably install air-conditioning and heating systems in your office as a matter of course. It is necessary, though, to understand the contrast between your office environment and the home environment of your staff, and the implications this may have. Many expats make a point of visiting the homes of their staff as a warm and team-building gesture, but are shocked to discover an absence of air-conditioning or heating. The situation gets worse as one moves north of the Yangtze, but most homes in Beijing are reasonably well-provided with such amenities. Shanghai, almost as cold, is not officially regarded as requiring heating in winter, particularly in the government offices. The propensity of local staff to sleep at their desks increases with the severity of the climate, as their homes are either too hot or too cold to get a good night's sleep. The only time they're comfortable is when they're at work. It can be a good idea to make inquiries in a supportive and caring way about the living conditions of your staff, with a view to minimizing the inevitable decline in productivity at certain times of the year.

Surviving business trips

The cities in China are so different that one visiting expatriate, on a trip to China to make preparations to relocate from the United States to Beijing, considered a side trip to Shanghai. She asked, 'Do they have the same currency in Shanghai?' Her 17-year-old daughter, embarrassed and irritated, responded, 'Mother, are you retarded?', but in fact the question was not so dumb as it may have appeared. Shanghai and Beijing are so different they may be on different planets, and the contrast between the prosperous southern coastal region and the rather primitive interior is even greater.

When travelling within China, it can a good idea to assume that you *are* on another planet, and not make any assumptions. One needs to appreciate the 'One country, several systems' concept; don't expect where you're going to be in any way similar to where you've just been. To say, 'Oh, we don't do this in Shanghai!' or 'In Beijing, we have *quite* a different approach' (especially if this implies that Shanghai or Beijing may be superior to where you are), is probably a mistake. People in China are immensely patriotic about their localities, a point made already. They will enjoy telling stories making fun of people in different parts of China, in the same way that Europeans and Americans tell jokes at the expense of people from other regions who they regard as stupid, mean, boring or displaying any other behaviour that presents others with opportunities for humour. If you laugh with them and add your own stories to supplement theirs, you'll have made friends—always a good approach in any business dealings.

Keep your sense of humour
Be prepared to cope with frustrations and don't be surprised at strange happenings. Try to be amused rather than annoyed at the ironies and bizarre happenings of travel in China. These two true stories are perhaps best saved for expatriate dinner party conversation only. The first story concerns a foreign traveller (FT) who is checking in at Shanghai for a flight to Beijing. FT has loaded three bags onto the luggage chute and is speaking to one of the airline staff (AS).

FT   *I'm checking in these three bags for Beijing.*
AS   That's RMB 30, please.
FT   *What for?*
AS   Insurance.
FT   *On what?*
AS   These three bags, RMB 10 each.
FT   *Since when?*
AS   New regulation.
FT   *So how much is the insured amount?*
AS   It says on the insurance ticket, RMB 5000 per item of luggage.
FT   *But my stuff is not worth that much!*
AS   New regulation. All checked-in baggage.
FT   *What if I don't pay?*
AS   Bags not allowed to be checked in.
FT   *OK, I'll carry them on the plane.*
AS   Not allowed, they're too big.

The second story is about an expatriate traveller (ET) waiting at an airport in the waiting room. He speaks to the room attendant (RA).

ET *Excuse me, Miss.*
RA Yes sir, can I help you?
ET *I thought this is a non-smoking area.*
RA Yes, sir.
ET *Is that sign there saying 'no smoking'?*
RA Yes, sir.
ET *Then why are those men sitting there smoking?*
RA Oh, that's OK, sir, they are our staff.

Anticipate airline problems

Since lateness of flights and long delays have become a way of life in China, it is essential that you give yourself leeway in making appointments at the other end. For foreigners unable to understand much Chinese, and travelling unaccompanied, the unpredictability of air travel and the inconveniences can take on nightmarish proportions. Other passengers are more likely to tell you what's going on than any airline officials. In fact, it's a good idea to make contact with any friendly looking locals heading for the same flight. Those wearing T-shirts or sweatshirts bearing the logo of any large multinational are likely to be friendly and speak English.

One non-Chinese-speaking expat was delighted when one such fellow passenger volunteered to help her with her excess baggage by taking some of her boxes onto his ticket, thereby much reducing the excess baggage charge (which is double for non-PRC nationals).

Useful guidelines are: fly early in the morning, on a plane from an airline based at your port of embarkation—with luck the plane is there ready and waiting; add at least one hour after estimated arrival time when scheduling your first meeting; call the person you'll be meeting from the airport departure lounge when you've ascertained that the flight is on time; get to the airport early if you have a lot of baggage to check in, as overweight baggage processing is time-consuming; have everything you need written down for you in Chinese, if necessary; and bring your own food and a can of soft drink in case of an emergency. Actually, food served on Chinese flights is improving. Something that provokes genuine panic is the sight of the airline serving dinner in the departure lounge. Then you have no idea when the flight will take off, if at all.

Accept all offers of help

Travelling is a very good way to meet people and to further distribute the ubiquitous *mingpian*. Always accept invitations to share taxis, not just for purposes of economy but because your new-found travelling companion probably knows the area better than you do and also has the potential to handle taxi drivers better. Two people travelling together are less likely to be ripped off than one alone. And all kinds of introductions can be useful. Keep a name-card file for each place you visit regularly; store introductions to use them in the future if you don't need them now. Overseas Chinese need no introduction to the importance of *guanxi*; foreigners learn very quickly.

Learn to avoid overindulgence at banquets

All guides to working and living in China abound with advice about surviving banquets and other forms of customer/supplier entertainment. The good news is that they aren't as frequent as they used to be, especially for meetings that are not at the highest level. In fact, government officials in Shanghai were banned from entertaining guests at the municipality's expense in late 1995. (On the day this ban was announced, an expat executive with a car distribution company in Shanghai was invited to such a function. He remarked that he didn't know who was paying for the banquet, but it wouldn't be him!)

The *Beijing Scene Guidebook* gives some useful advice. 'During every proper banquet there is a fish course. Five minutes after the fish arrives, you should initiate the business conversation. The goal of the fish course is to raise areas of concern and seek agreement on matters of principle. Regardless of the results, retreat into pleasantries before finishing the noodles or rice...and the fruit is for joke time.'

Keep trips to a minimum
Travelling in China can be tiring and immensely time-consuming. Another drawback to being on the road is that it reduces the time available to you to make progress with staff training back at your home base. Use your business trips to make contacts so that future business can be conducted as much as possible by telephone. In the early days following your arrival, spend as much time as you can with your staff to build up their skills and level of motivation, and keep any business trips as short as possible. Fly at weekends, very early in the morning or in the evening in order to minimize time out of the office, especially in those crucial early months.

As time goes by, try and reduce the number and frequency of your business trips, not only to give you the chance to concentrate on operations at your home base but to conserve energy.

Keep your staff busy while you're away
Constant travelling on your part can be disastrous if staff are untrained and little progress has been made in teaching empowerment and responsibility. In such a situation, no decisions, even of the most minor nature, will be made unless you happen to telephone in and ask if your help is needed. Avoid the office grinding to a halt in your absence by preparing your staff beforehand: give them clear job objectives, clear task deadlines, and clear rewards and punishments if jobs are done or not done.

In China, there is a popular tendency for local staff to ease off when the boss is not around—the 'while the cat's away' syndrome. Get them used to the idea that it's not you who's generating the work, it's the business—getting customers, filling orders, negotiating with suppliers and so on, and that this goes on whether you are there or not. Develop a regular routine for them, if the nature of your work allows it. Draw up a list of processes and procedures that are to be completed regularly, put it in writing and ensure everyone has a copy. It is preferable if the staff are involved with the compilation of this and their input sought, as this gives them a sense of ownership.

Being an entrepreneur in China

Dan Shao insists that a pioneering, 'Go West!' spirit is the best mentality for preparing to work as an entrepreneur in China. You need to understand the benefits and rewards, but also be clear on the challenges. 'There are many things you'll miss here, and the living environment is in great contrast with the comforts of the US, but you just need to get over this, and not let it worry you. China must be seen as an adventure, and a place where you can make an impact!'

Understand the environment

Entrepreneurs in the United States can find a much easier environment than in China. Whereas the US entrepreneurial environment is relatively free and open, the China market seems strange and dominated by insecurity and uncertainty. Shao says, 'Entrepreneurs need the right environment to succeed, and China, while offering great opportunities, is more challenging. There are more rules and regulations, whereas in the US, if you have a dream, you can go ahead and do it. In China, there are more obstacles, and it's more of an adventure. It's harder to be successful as an entrepreneur in China, but there are more opportunities. In the US, it's the other way around. In some ways, China is like King Solomon's mines—but a lot of people have lost a lot of money as well as making a lot.'

Experienced China entrepreneurs also point out that you should not undercapitalize your operation, because it may take longer than you expect to show results, and you need to keep going in the meantime. Do things properly—get a work permit, and ideally work from an office rather than from home. If you run a small operation, aim for a clearly defined niche position rather than trying to be everything to all customers. It's also important to make the distinction between an investor and an entrepreneur—being one of the latter, you can't come and go, you are much more committed.

Kathy Bao of Chung Shing is an entrepreneur and an investor in China, but sees herself as active and committed. 'Of those investing money in China, around 90 per cent just leave it and go home. They've given up. You can never be successful if you come and go. And China is so big. The more you put in, there's always more you can put in. Even if we are successful, it's only in such a small part of China. There is always so much more. You have to keep going, and you can't just leave it to manage itself.'

Many China-based entrepreneurs have to understand that it may be more difficult to hire local staff, who are often attracted to large multinationals and who think that small newly established businesses are more risky. As an entrepreneur, you must also decide if the business will be personal to you, if you want to build a sustainable business for the future—will it be limited to China or does it have the potential to be bigger? Is it now the China branch of a bigger enterprise? Be sure to get advice from those who've done it already, especially in the China market.

Beware the ambitious around you
Philip Chan, who was working in the insurance industry in Shenzhen, finds that the local fascination with the stock-market tends to deflect local staff from their purpose of working in a corporate business. The stock-market, which has spawned many local entrepreneurs, is luring local staff away. 'They think they can make a fast buck this way. All they know is a bull market, so they think it's easy to make money, and that you can do this rather than doing a job. If they have a job, they do this investing on the side. As an employer, you have to be careful, because this can become more interesting to them than their job.'

Managing costs and revenues

As Johnny Ho explains, things can cost more in China than many China investors realize. 'Even if you are reasonably generous with salaries, staff costs are still a small part of the overall costs. And manufacturing costs are also quite low here.' However, a lot of things cost a great deal more than one might imagine, and it is essential to establish control mechanisms from the outset.

Watch the costs

'What is expensive,' Ho says, 'is the continuing need to import raw materials, from the US and Europe. I expect it will take around three to five years to produce many of the raw materials we need. Take packaging, for example. An Australian joint venture here is making bottles which are a lot better than the completely local ones, but they are still not good enough. The quality of sand available in China is very poor.'

Realize, also, that your pay and housing may be one of the largest cost elements, and can put a greater obligation on you to make money quickly. As Ho confirms, 'Another huge cost is that of expats like myself. My home costs a great deal in rental each month. This is not at all unusual in Shanghai. My costs are more than the whole payroll.'

Just about everything consumed by expatriates costs more than it would for locals—this is something to be borne in mind when local staff compare their salaries with those of expats, as discussed above. In particular, local housing is rarely an option for an expat. In Shanghai it can be possible, but in Beijing, foreigners and overseas Chinese are limited to strictly delineated housing areas. Outside the major cities in China, expat housing is extremely limited, and most find themselves living in hotel rooms or suites.

Try for profits early

If you can, try and generate profit as soon as possible after arrival in China. This will calm your boss's nerves as well as enhance your image at head office. When **Thu Ho** took over at Shanghai RAAS Blood Products, a joint venture involving California-based Rare Antibody Antigen Supply Inc., making blood derivatives products for the local market, the US partner wanted to make the business productive straight away, and start bringing in money immediately. So, before manufacturing started, the joint venture imported products from Europe and from elsewhere to get the salesforce up and running, to start generating profits and to keep the Chinese joint venture partner happy. 'We hired a dozen or so doctors to be the core of the salesforce,' explains Ho. 'They had no previous sales experience; we had to train them. So even before we had our own products to sell, we got started this way.'

Budget for staff costs

Local staff in China commonly receive benefits unheard of in many other countries—for housing, meals, clothes, transport, visits to parents and spouses, as well as for medical costs, children's education and insurance. Consult your local human resources staff or a consultant before preparing your budgets.

Chapter 2

Setting up your team

O ne of the first tasks of the newly arrived executive is to put together a team of local staff. Whether you find them through advertising the jobs, a job fair, networking or head-hunting, you want the right people who will comfortably fit into your corporate culture. You also want people who will stay.

Recruiting the right people

Many PRC locals fundamentally mistrust foreign companies and still cling to the iron rice bowl offered by the State sector. So even if they do join a foreign company, they may be thinking of only a short forage into the unknown—mostly for the sake of a larger salary—before retreating once more to the security of a State-Owned Enterprise (SOE).

Even if Chinese staff in a multinational never go back to an SOE, they may still regard employment with a foreign company as being only temporary and carry on promiscuously flitting around between jobs. As Hong Kong head-hunter Martin Tang commented, 'It used to be that Hong Kong people were always job-hopping. Now the mainland staff are even more mobile than them.' So finding someone to join your company and commit to you will not be easy.

Find people who will stay

Anne Ng, who is with an international firm of head-hunters in Shanghai, maintains somewhat cynically that it's impossible to find people who will stay. She maintains that everything militates against their long-term sojourn in your organization—there is the desire to return to an SOE with all its perks, the chance of being head-hunted to join another multinational which will pay more, the possibility of leaving China to emigrate or study or of returning to another part of China to take care of sick relatives, and even of leaving the corporate sector to become an entrepreneur. All things are possible.

Finding people who will stay is one of the biggest challenges of all, agrees **Jim King**. He says, 'There's a distinct shortage of people in China who will plan to stay on a long-term basis in a foreign company. They just don't think this way yet.' Many PRC locals are convinced that foreign companies are here today and gone tomorrow, and they do have evidence for this (some, but not much). As described above, foreign companies are often seen as salary cash-cows, to be milked before moving on to another, with an increase in salary to be gained at each move. People with this kind of mind-set must be identified and avoided.

An even greater challenge to the employer are the people who don't really think this way but who are constantly being approached by head-hunters facing a highly restricted pool of potential candidates. Such people find it hard to say 'no': many are strongly influenced by spouses, parents and university professors who may be ill-informed and mercenary, and don't take long-term career plans into consideration. This is not surprising—'career-planning' is a new concept in China, where most university graduates expect to be allocated to work units not of their own choosing. Even the very concept of choice is new to China.

'Yet,' Jim King explains, 'it's not surprising that local people feel some insecurity in a foreign company. They don't know much about them. They have different values and attitudes towards staff. Local people really do worry that the foreign companies may go out of business.'

This fear is understandable when one realizes that many SOEs are losing money. At a British Embassy briefing in mid-1996, it was revealed that total aggregate profits of SOEs were down 70 per cent from 1995, and total aggregate losses had increased by 50 per cent. Many of the SOEs are now paying staff RMB 100 a month to stay at home and not come to work. PRC people don't know a lot about the profitability of foreign companies or the extent of their commitment to investing money in the PRC—such information isn't easily available. Why should foreign companies be different from SOEs? Also, they don't offer any promise to continue to provide for staff if the business goes bust. Staff would be laid off, perhaps without even the RMB 100 a month.

There is another factor, too. Jim King says, 'Government policies towards foreign companies may change dramatically, at short notice, and of course we all worry about this. However, I try to preach to my staff the benefits of having a long-term philosophy in your career and how loyalty to a company is highly prized by all employers; I look for people who are receptive to this.' The fact that many multinationals have for several years been successful in China is helping to make people feel less insecure, and in fact it is now widely believed that a job in a large and well-capitalized multinational could be more secure than a job in the SOE sector, where large numbers of people are being laid off. The streets are now filling up with small-time entrepreneurs, selling lunch-boxes or mending shoes, who are trying to supplement their RMB 100 a month. Word is getting around that the iron rice bowl is finally being broken. People who have the potential to be hired by a multinational are beginning to realize they have less and less to lose by making this leap into the unknown.

Mark Thomas comments that hotels were among the first overseas enterprises to set up in China, and were immediately attractive to local employees. 'Around five or so years ago, it was easy to get high-quality local employees for foreign hotels. The hotels could hire graduates from some of the best universities and not pay them much. But now, as the economy has expanded, there is more choice for these people.' Hotels became a favourite poaching ground for newly arrived foreign companies looking for staff, and now many of the most highly paid jobs are outside the hotel industry.

Thomas now prefers to hire junior staff at lower salaries and give them lots of opportunities to improve by, for example, teaching them English and good customer service skills. 'For example, I promoted a locker room attendant to a receptionist's position. Some of the customers complained because she couldn't speak English very well, but she is now getting on quite well, and she clearly valued the opportunity. If I had a smart graduate who spoke good English, he or she would just get poached very quickly by the members and guests.' Thomas's work is paying off in terms of developing loyalty and team spirit.

Comparing his Hong Kong and China experiences, Thomas feels that expats in Hong Kong just see the place as an extension of home and behave in very much the same way as they would at home. 'In the PRC, the differences and contrasts are much clearer, it's all so different, there's more of a deliberate change in behaviour. Many expats get into a rut easily in Hong Kong, but this is impossible in China!'

Thomas actually had more staff problems in Hong Kong than he has had in China. 'We had such high staff turnover in Hong Kong; we've been able to develop a stronger sense of staff loyalty here. Once you win people's hearts here, they will stay with you and you can get this long-term commitment. But you can't move too fast—it takes time, like around a year, to get people to feel loyal to you.'

So, as a solution to the problem of a shortage of people who will stay, expat executives are advised to encourage long-term commitment: emphasize the advantages of company loyalty, particularly loyalty to your company, and the opportunities now offered by foreign companies in China, compared with the uncertainties of an SOE. And make it clear that job-hopping eventually leads to no job, because foreigners in recruiting mode are, above all, looking for stability and reliability.

Applicants with laundry lists of company names and job titles on their resumes will soon find themselves receiving the cold shoulder. 'I was presented with the CV of a young lady looking for a job which showed that she'd had seven jobs already, and she was still under 30 years old,' commented Shanghai-based head-hunter, Henry Yung. 'Not only had she worked for totally different companies, her jobs had been in administration, secretarial, marketing, human resources—even management information services. Her CV made no sense. But she was quite arrogant, thinking she was really rather special. Many of the jobs she'd stayed in for only three months, then she'd decided she didn't like the company or her co-workers. This is also a common tendency in China. These people know they're sought-after, so if they decide they don't like their job, they just leave and get another. They think it's that easy. But they are beginning to learn that they can run out of luck, and meanwhile their track record of job-hopping has damaged their future prospects.'

Some high-flying young PRC executives, including those who have acquired one of the prestigious foreign qualifications now available inside China (such as from the China Europe International Business School, or CEIBS), don't actually recognize good companies offering excellent long-term prospects when they come across them. 'I've had an offer from McKinsey, from BCG, from Procter & Gamble, and from Kraft,' said one such graduate to a Hong Kong journalist who writes on career matters. 'Are these good companies? I don't know. Maybe I should send my CV to the head-hunters. Which head-hunters should I send it to?' When told that these were all excellent companies with whom one could profitably spend several years or even one's entire career, and that head-hunters were only interested in qualified executives with several years of experience, they were not convinced.

Learn how to keep staff

Which companies in your sector are most successful at keeping staff and what do they do to achieve this success? What specific long-term strategies and/or short-term techniques do they employ? It's worth building relationships with other companies so that, if appropriate, you can learn tips from them and use the principles of their successful strategies as bench-marks for your own approach. In China, many expats find that the disadvantages of opening yourself up to your competitors are far outweighed by the advantages of sharing information and experiences. Everyone is in the same boat, but it's a big boat, so there's still room for everyone on board.

Companies who are successful in retaining staff have spent a lot of time helping new recruits to understand the company culture, and the reasons why the company is special. These staff members have become immersed in the company's values, and the company has become their family. They are convinced of the company's long-term future in China and of the security of their jobs, and they have a clear picture of their rewarding and continually growing career in the company.

Shell is a good example of a company with an excellent track record of retaining staff. From the late 1980s to 1996, out of over 100 members of staff in Shanghai, Shell has lost only eight, mostly because their spouses wanted to migrate. One man left to join a competitor, only to return a few months later asking for his old job back and bringing with him two colleagues from his former company who turned out to be excellent workers!

How does Shell do it? Training is partly responsible—each member of staff in Shanghai is offered up to 15–20 days a year of management and supervisory skills training (over and above technical skills training) at an annual cost of up to US$200,000 per hundred staff members. However, no training or other perks are offered until the person has been satisfactorily working at Shell for over a year, and is therefore judged to be committed to the company. The company also takes care to select 'Shell' people—those who it feels will fit in happily and will be receptive to the company culture. Many of these people are newly qualified graduates with good degrees who've never worked for anyone else. If the head-hunters call them, they are quite capable of saying, 'Why should I want to work anywhere else when I work for Shell?' Shell's structured approach to training is described in greater detail in Chapter 4 on pages 140–142.

Other companies enjoying such enviably loyal workforces include ABB and Motorola. Their staff are aggressively proud of their *mingpian*s and derive great status and face from their employing company—they see themselves as far above the inferior beings in other companies. For many foreign companies, this is certainly one way to retain staff; however, as their boss, you have to deal with these frequently arrogant people on a day-to-day basis. There are other drawbacks, too. Their unquestioning loyalty can mean that they lack critical faculties; they can be intensely conservative; and they can lack any kind of entrepreneurial spirit, ambition or drive (probably due to the fact that they are very 'comfortable'). Equally significant is the likelihood that they lack the experience and insights which can be gained by working in other companies.

The following example serves as an illustration. In one public training workshop, a participant approached the organizer and said, 'I work for Motorola, and I think your training is quite good', as if the status of her employer gave her unique credentials to pass judgement on an outside supplier. Perhaps she was surprised that anything not from Motorola was actually tolerable in quality.

Besides the corporate culture indoctrination method, specific benefits are used by many companies to encourage a longer-term attitude from staff. In the hotel industry, especially, seniority bonuses are awarded—extra pay for each quarter or even each month worked—which accumulate over a period to amount to a substantial sum. Like Shell, some companies only offer training to long-staying staff; the drawback to this approach, however, is that training is regarded as a reward and not as a method to develop skills and motivation. Training should support and advance the company's overall and long-term objectives, not be seen as a variation on bonuses and company incentives. The important thing is to understand what motivates each key staff member and use this knowledge to retain them, or at least make them think twice about saying 'yes' when the head-hunter calls.

Craig Pepples confirms the success of using a long-term bonus incentive method. 'It's crass, but it works. Bonuses keep people—they don't leave so readily. But I also try to emphasize the other attractions besides money. "What do you like about working here?" I ask them. I encourage them to think about how much they can learn, the new skills they can gain, the new people they can meet, which can mean more to them than the money they can earn each month. We've now got people who I know will stay, because they've thought about other things, not just about the money. I would advise managers, in recruiting staff, to look for those who fit in with the values of their organization. For example, our values are to be lean and mean but to encourage self-learning and self-inventing. We have lost some staff because they think the working conditions are too poor. They want a nice desk and nice computer. They won't get them here. But they will get excitement, a fast pace, a chance to share ideas—even the most outrageous ideas. Not everyone will want this, so we look for people who do want this. Other companies are quite different.'

Pepples's policy for finding people who will stay (explained further below) is to hire young people who will 'grow up' with the company. He says, 'This is our policy all over Asia. Particularly in China, it can be better not to go with older people who can't change and can't learn.

As with many other companies, we'll hire young people who fit in with the culture of the company and use them as a resource, moving between jobs within the company. We always want to make internal appointments, to keep and develop people who know how the company works. This also addresses their desire to move on and get advancement. They have a sense of entitlement, that there comes a time when they feel they can hit the jackpot, and you have to bear this in mind and keep giving them opportunities.'

Craig Pepples favours hiring young staff from State-owned enterprises who can be moulded and developed. 'They can become more loyal, because you've given them an opportunity, which perhaps other people would not give them. It's very rewarding to see them blossom, to see their world become bigger. These rough diamonds can be polished, but it takes time. You would give yourself a nervous breakdown if you expected their progress to go along at the same pace as in a more developed market. But at the same time, you need them to progress more quickly than they can, because in China we're always short of good staff and the normal development period for supervisors and junior managers has to be accelerated.'

Rough diamonds among your China staff are not just young people from State-owned enterprises. They can be young people without university qualifications or people from poorer parts of China who have migrated to the larger cities. They're already tough, because they've had to face discrimination from arrogant Shanghainese and Beijingers. They'll particularly appreciate an expat who gives them a chance.

Michael Wu sums it up by saying, 'There's no secret way to staff retention; I just try to be fair, to be caring, to provide a sense of belonging. If there's anything I've done that works, it's been that I've provided a family atmosphere, a feeling of being at home, with the family, that this hotel is not just a place where they come to work. How do I do this? Mostly by team-building employee activities. We have started an employee council in the hotel, organized by the employees. We've had ping-pong matches, soccer, karaoke, sponsored walks and an arts festival with a dance contest and photography contest. The staff actively join in these activities, look forward to them, talk about them—it gives them a common interest and sense of belonging. We've also created a staff recreation room in the hotel.'

Wu also makes proficiency in work skills an activity for competition between staff. He gives out cash prizes of around RMB 500–1000—not much in money terms but still worth winning—for staff who show outstanding competence in such things as making beds, laying tables, setting up a function room and typing menus, based on accuracy, efficiency and speed. 'We've also had an English speech-giving contest, especially to emphasize our English language teaching in the hotel.'

Wu considers that the staff retention situation is becoming easier, especially in the hotel business. 'Not only are there more things happening in the hotel to keep people, but there are definitely fewer opportunities available on the outside, as the economy has slowed down. Our staff turnover is much reduced since 1992–93.'

There were times in the early 1990s, especially in the Special Economic Zone, when staff turnover in hotels was as high as 25 per cent *per month*, which meant that every four months almost every member of staff in the hotel was different. One area which still suffers from a high rate of turnover is reception and front-desk work, where proficiency in English is required. Wu says, 'If a staff member speaks good English, inevitably they will prefer a 9–5 job to working in a hotel, so we'll always lose people here, probably.' To counteract this problem, Wu plans to install a voice-mail system in each guest room in the hotel, for message-taking.

One of Mark Thomas's staff members made a significant comment. 'When you first come to live in China, things seem quite simple, but the longer you are here, the more complicated you find things actually are.' This is especially true of attempts made to retain staff, such as building relationships, training and giving instructions. Thomas says, 'You can't just tell someone to do something but, since you don't want to be working all the hours your organization is open, you have to find a way of building trust, of helping people to manage themselves. First of all, you have to prove yourself to them, that you can do the job, so that they can respect you. When I arrived to work at the club, there was an assistant manager who'd been here around seven years, and all the staff looked to him for instructions. So I had to prove myself to the staff independently of him. When he left to join another hotel, it was easier; then I could run it all on my own.'

Thomas also says, 'The most common mistake I see being made here in China is by expats wanting to change things overnight. They behave like a bull in a China shop. They are inevitably destructive and resented by the locals, who will then quickly leave.'

Select your staff carefully

Lee Swee Chee finds people who will fit into his organization and who have potential, then he trains them so that ultimately they will take over the recruitment work. Lee is in charge of all hiring and has developed a policy of careful selection to ensure his organization obtains the most appropriate staff. He has now been able to delegate a lot of the day-to-day management, including some of the hiring. 'I was very proactive and hands-on in my hiring policy when we first started. I hired everyone myself at the beginning. I was looking for people with the right qualifications but I was, above all, looking for the right attitude. I wanted people who could take ownership of their jobs, which is very much part of the culture of Honeywell.'

Lee wanted to create a working environment where people would be active and busy, and not idle. 'I've found that if people are idle, the office politics intensify, people gossip and complain about each other, and the whole place degenerates.' Local staff, especially those with long experience of working in an SOE, are used to a level of underemployment not tolerated by most multinationals.

Lee's objective after setting up the initial team was to promote the better members so that they could then hire people themselves: however, this stage has just been reached, the process having taken up most of the last four years. 'When I first arrived, we had just 10–15 people who were a liaison group working with the Beijing office. Then I started hiring people, who initially all reported to me. But you can't go on like that for long, as it would just be too large for such a flat organization. Now we have more than 100 people in Shanghai, and a corporate structure based on local managers working on their own initiative, and hiring their own staff.'

Daniel Chieh, a Chinese from Taiwan who manages a multinational sales and marketing operation in Shanghai, did the same. 'I hired all my own staff. My family complained because for several months I spent all my Saturdays doing this. But it was absolutely necessary to find the right people.' It also took Chieh years, training and developing his local staff, before he felt able to delegate this task.

Mark Gau uses the concept of mutual respect to explain the values of his company when he's hiring new staff. Respect for individuals, reasonableness and fairness are emphasized as the dominant features of his company's code of conduct. And he wants people who will fit into that culture. When he's looking for new staff, he's likely to look for skills first, building from that into developing a spirit of team-work. Gau would rather just have competent people with the potential to be moulded into good team players, people with skills who can be brought into the team later.

'I always interview staff along with my joint venture partner, and I know they're thinking about how this person will fit in, while I concentrate on their skills. I always take a lot of advice from the joint venture partner. If they say the person is too expensive and may not fit in, I would

71

accept this, if I couldn't reach a compromise. Imagine if I hired someone in contravention of the joint venture partner's advice? Then this person would become "a Mark Gau person", not an equal member of the team and, if I wasn't around, that person would have no status.'

For this reason, training others up to a level where they are competent to take on a lot of the hiring work is very important. Then company responsibility is seen as shared, and not dominated by expats. When local people can hire other local people, this marks an important transitional achievement.

Learn what motivates your staff
Why do your staff work for you? You probably can't ask them this question directly, but you need to know the answer. You may not get a straight answer even if you did ask it, but you still need some response. Any answers you do get can be taken into account when you consider what incentives to offer your staff. You also need to know how some of the more common motivators can strongly affect the behaviour of your staff.

For example, staff motivated by money will be most excited at the thought of a bonus or pay rise so, to make the most of this excitement, they should be working on a commission or performance-related pay basis. However, such people are are more likely to be lured away by another company willing to pay more, and it's hard for you to build loyalty to a pay packet alone.

Staff motivated by status will get a kick out of working for what they regard as a 'classy' company and will talk about how 'low class' other companies are by comparison. They love to give out their name-cards to their friends and show off about their boss, their office location, their company's image or anything that they think enhances their own image. A chance to accompany their boss to a high-profile social gathering will give them a huge buzz. These people are often not interested in work as such, are not productive and are not commercially minded.

Although staff motivated by the opportunity to learn may also not be very business-minded and may be quite academic in orientation, they are, by definition, trainable! They are most happy at the thought of going off to a seminar or attending a course, and those genuinely keen on learning will make the most of the classes and implement what they learnt.

There are many different attitudes to training, especially public training, and training opportunities are popular among those influenced by each of the three motivational factors discussed here. For example, training can be used to meet other employers to get a new job to make more money; training can prove that one's boss thinks one is important enough to send on a training course; and training is, of course, an opportunity to learn. Those motivated by the opportunity to learn will also be happy to have a chance to run a training class themselves one day. But they must always be encouraged to implement their new skills, to break out of the academic mould, and see that training is not just training for its own sake, but that it has benefits further down the track.

According to **Johnny Ho**, one of the most difficult recruitment areas is sales. Although this is a key role, it's a weak area for many China staff—not because they can't do it, but because they don't want to. 'We need about 40–50 salespeople, but only three or four marketing people. But no-one wants to go into sales; they all want to go into marketing. Because sales is seen as low-status, it tends to attract the least able people. So you must concentrate on incentivizing them and building up their self-respect. I do this partly by paying a larger base salary and lower proportion of commission, to give them more security. I'll pay them 70 per cent salary and 30 per cent commission. In Hong Kong and Taiwan, it's liable to be 50/50, or even less salary. In China, you have to guarantee them a stable income to keep them. The turnover of staff in my salesforce is much lower than it is in many other companies. And as they're promoted, I increase their commission and keep their base salary. I offer salespeople good incentives, such as cash prizes and training seminars, and I give them the best tools for the job—uniforms, beepers and motorbikes.'

On the other hand, Ho points out the strengths, the best features, of a typical Chinese workforce. 'There are very good universities here, with people excellent in such things as mechanics, engineering and maths. It's not surprising they're not so good at sales—they haven't had much commercial experience. But I have been quite successful in turning technical people into good salespeople. I have a sign on the office wall in big Chinese characters: "All you need to be a successful salesperson is hard work and honesty". You don't need to be a genius, you just need to be polite to the customers and build a good relationship with them. The only difference is in attitude. If you find a person who is hard-working and honest, they can do well.

Some salespeople go out with their girlfriend or boyfriend and invent their sales reports, but they can't fool you for long. In fact, people who are too clever don't last. They get bored, and they get bigger offers from elsewhere. Also, they don't have patience, they take short cuts, and they always want promotion.'

Many local staff in China working for a big brand-name company feel that this gives them a huge amount of prestige. They think that the respect accorded them is for themselves as individuals; they don't realize it is largely for the brand name. When they want to change jobs, they think they can retain the prestige and make more money in the process. They would do well to remember the proverb about the fox assuming the tiger's might:

> When a tiger caught a fox while looking for his prey, the fox tried to persuade him that he should not be eaten, on the grounds that he, the fox, was king of the beasts and protected by the Emperor of Heaven. To convince the tiger, the fox insisted that if he led the way, with the tiger following close behind, the tiger would see that all the animals would flee at the sight of the fox. As the two of them set off, all the other animals did indeed flee—and the tiger thought it was because they were afraid of the fox.

'The fox assumes the tiger's might' (Chinese proverb, Zhanguo Ce)

Don't forget the impact of recent history

An expatriate with the responsibility of recruiting and promoting local staff in China would do well to understand the impact the Cultural Revolution had on people there, and also the significance of the concept of the iron rice bowl. **Kathy Bao** of Chung Shing has found that, in recruiting and promoting staff, local staff in their mid-30s or above are struggling to overcome their missed education and to reach middle management levels. 'Now people in their 20s have better prospects to climb faster,' Bao comments. 'The younger people are stealing a march on the older staff, the "lost generation" of China. Especially someone in their 20s with foreign-language skills, a university degree and computer knowledge—they have much more opportunity to progress now than ever before. Foreign companies now want younger people, and staff in their late 30s and 40s are not in demand; they don't have the necessary experience, they missed out because of what was happening in China at the time.'

Bao sees problems in a situation where younger staff are favoured and the older staff lack experience. 'Young people in China as a whole don't look up to their elders and pay respect to them in the way that they do in Taiwan, for example. And this means that younger people in China, generally speaking, think they are much more capable and knowledgeable than they really are. And they are unstable, with a tendency towards job-hopping. They have a high opinion of themselves, no sense of loyalty, little experience, and know nothing about managing people.'

So, despite their lack of experience, Bao would often prefer to encourage and promote the middle-aged people on her staff. 'They are easy to satisfy, their expectations are not so high, and they are more stable.' As the textile industry is still quite low-tech, 'We don't need such a high level of education. Older people can do well here and they know how to handle the local people, better than our Taiwan staff can. Those older people, in their 40s and 50s, who survived the Cultural Revolution, are very sharp and give us good advice on how to solve our people-management problems here. We have three or four people like this here.

'We would like to promote more local staff to senior management positions but it's difficult. We try to use as many local people as we can, and source them for new positions. We use recommendations from existing experienced, trustworthy staff because, as a rule, good people don't respond to newspaper ads and it's easier to get them by recommendation,' Bao explains.

Craig Pepples also remarks on how the Cultural Revolution distorted the lives of people, and has affected both the older and younger generations. 'Certainly, young people in China don't respect their parents so much, but a foreign company can help bridge the gap by giving status to both older and younger people. We mostly hire younger people, but we have some senior staff who did experience this period in China's history. Older people can be nostalgic about the Cultural Revolution, amazingly enough, despite the hardships they suffered. Younger people don't know much about it, except what they've heard from their parents. Foreigners like myself are fascinated by the Cultural Revolution, and I like to sing "The East is Red" at our company social functions. The younger staff are perplexed and embarrassed—they're more interested in the future. But those who survived the Cultural Revolution can have fine qualities—many of which the Cultural Revolution tried to destroy. Some have great wisdom, maturity and leadership skills. By contrast, there's a lack of humility in the younger generation now.'

The iron rice bowl concept tends to encourage an attitude of 'Now I have a job, they will carry on paying my salary, whether I do anything or not' in the minds of the staff. Members of staff with this mind-set will be surprised when called to task for poor performance, and when told they are not suitable in their job, will expect to be given another job of their choosing elsewhere in the company. Whether or not that job exists, whether or not that task is needed, whether that individual is making a contribution to the profits of the company or not—all this is irrelevant. They consider that it is the company's duty to provide for them. 'Think not what your company can do for you, but what you can do for your company' is a paraphrase that makes sense to many multinational employers. Many PRC Chinese simply cannot grasp such a concept.

Beware of staff members who think they might like to go to the United States and study for an MBA, don't know if they can get a visa or not, and yet ask you if you will hold their jobs open for them while the immigration authorities think about it. Of course, if they get a visa, they will leave the next day and you will be one staff member short...but they don't want you to look for a replacement, just in case they want to keep their job after all. Be firm—the iron rice bowl does not exist in foreign companies. It won't exist in Chinese companies for much longer, either, if the growth of the Chinese economy is to be maintained.

Avoid nepotism

In some factories and work units, the iron rice bowl goes further—you not only have a job for life, it carries on to your offspring or relatives after your retirement or death! As **Thu Ho** describes it, many staff expect the company to do everything for them, including passing jobs on to their successors.

'A friend of mine running a joint venture in Shanghai attended the funeral of one of his staff who had died. This person had died of natural causes, nothing to do with the company. But the next day, this staff member's wife came to his office, asking for a job. It's like she believed that he'd had a right to a job in this company, so it meant that she could inherit that right, since he had died. It's like the practices of the Chinese work unit being transferred to a foreign company. My friend refused. You can't allow such staff dependence on your company and stay commercially viable, but you must show that you care. So we have a fund, administered by the union, for making reasonable payments in such circumstances.'

The localization debate

Many Westerners and overseas Chinese are keen to recruit their fellow countrymen rather than local staff to management jobs. Paul Moran says that at his company, Siemens, a certain proportion of Western expats will always be required as 'local staff are just not ready for senior management roles, although we're reducing the proportion of expats and we're promoting locals up to more and more middle-management positions'.

Dominic Tang, a Hong Kong Chinese running a Sino–French joint venture, maintains that Westerners are not appropriate when it comes to running China operations 'because of their inability to communicate, and their lack of understanding about what's going on in China.

Even those who do speak Chinese are ignorant of how things get done here, and their staff can run rings around them too easily'.

Craig Pepples's operation has been highly localized since Day One. 'We just have a few Westerners, and no overseas Chinese. Some companies think you can take a person from Hong Kong or Taiwan, send them to China and they can just carry on. But in fact they need as much training as the Westerners. Many of the skills of a Hong Kong Chinese, for example, may be of no value in China. They have to go through a long learning process. We have found that it's better to hire bright young locals, train them up, and keep just the minimum number of Westerners in key positions, with the aim of localizing them sooner or later.'

Some large multinationals regard the hiring of overseas Chinese and the phasing out of Westerners as a step towards localization. When Westerners from head office arrive, all they see are Chinese faces, and they think, 'How progressive!'. But this can be a negative step. Some local staff become resentful and lose motivation when overseas Chinese are hired and paid many times their salaries (the salaries of overseas Chinese are usually on a par with those of Westerners) when, to them, basically they are all Chinese. The overseas Chinese in question tend to try to distance themselves from the local people and spend their time with other overseas Chinese and Westerners. Expat managers, to be successful, need to show their commitment to PRC Chinese staff by building close relationships with them, by supporting them, coaching them, training them, and building them into a team.

Cultural assimilation can be the hardest thing, maintains Craig Pepples. 'We needed to make an appointment in China, for a sales job in Beijing, and we scoured three continents. But we found the person we wanted in our own backyard. Sometimes it's easier to teach a person skills when he or she has the appropriate cultural sensitivities, than vice versa. It's like the restaurants with singing waiters. Do you find waiters and teach them to sing, or do you find singers and teach them to be waiters? Actually, you should decide which of the skills is harder to teach, find people with those skills already, then teach them the easier skills. I think cultural sensitivity to China is much harder to teach than selling, so I would rather hire local people and train them in how to be a salesperson. Many of them are natural salespeople anyway, they just need techniques and polish.'

To Westerners, the need for cultural assimilation is obvious. As Pepples describes it, 'There's not a moment in China when you think you're in Kansas! You're aware that the differences are huge. You really do know that you're on a different planet.' Local people do make allowances for you, don't necessarily expect you to be culturally attuned to them and can be quite impressed when you show you're trying. It's different for Hong Kong Chinese, Taiwanese and other overseas Chinese, including returnees. Their Chinese-ness can mask their differences. Pepples says, 'I've heard of Hong Kong people in China saying to local staff, "You're not doing what I want—you're stupid!", forgetting that they are speaking out of context. It might be fair to say that in your own culture, but not in someone else's.'

When hiring staff in China, it's easy to focus on faults rather than on strengths, and to have expectations of perfection which cannot be met. But it's possible to make a successful appointment by hiring a person who turns out to have good points which outweigh any faults that are initially apparent. On such an occasion, it's worth bearing in mind the story about looking at flowers while riding on horseback:

A young man who unfortunately was crippled and unable to walk, nevertheless had dreams of marrying a beautiful young girl. At the same time, a young girl who had an unattractive flat, snub nose wanted to find a handsome young man as her husband. They both called upon the same matchmaker, who decided to try and match them, without telling them of each other's faults. He arranged a meeting, having told the young man to ride a horse to hide his inability to walk, and having advised the young lady to stand at the doorway holding a spray of flowers, which would conceal her nose. The two young people liked the look of each other and decided to marry, only then discovering each other's faults. Nevertheless, they laughed them off, and had a good marriage.

'Enjoy looking at flowers while riding on horseback' (Chinese proverb, Jiutang Shu)

Handling dismissal procedures in China

The system of laying off staff—the quick decision, the firing, the clearing out of the desk and out of the door—as known in some Western business cultures is rarely appropriate in China. Staff must be able to keep face, to feel they can justify their departure, to have a story to tell the rest of the world. Craig Pepples suggests that a manager should have a discussion with the staff member in question, along the lines of 'Perhaps this job is not working for you...perhaps you're not really happy here. It may be possible to find a better place for your talents than here'.

'You should give them a way out,' he says. 'Outside China, you can divorce people from their job. They can get another job somewhere else. Companies laying off people tell them that their job has become redundant, not them. But in China, because of the tradition of jobs for life, people strongly identify with their jobs. So dispensing with their services has to be handled delicately. If they feel that they don't like their job any more or don't fit into the company, this is better than telling them that their performance is not acceptable, that they are no longer wanted. It can be too shocking to them personally.'

It's important in the China context to avoid letting go of a member of staff in such a way that they will hold a grudge against you and a thirst for vengeance. If someone is looking for dirt on another person or company in China, it's always possible to find it. With the ambiguities in the legal system and the loopholes in company operating regulations that exist in the PRC, 'No-one is entirely clean,' says Pepples, who tells the story of one company who closed itself down and opened a new one to avoid attempts at muck-raking by a revenge-seeking ex-employee who had been humiliatingly fired in front of fellow employees. This firing had been mishandled by a Hong Kong Chinese who failed to think through the needs of the local people and who had left the staff member concerned with no face-saving excuse or story.

'Many Westerners don't realize that Hong Kong people are much more exposed to the West than they are to

China, that China is another planet for them, and they don't necessarily make the right cultural assumptions,' says Pepples. Even Hong Kong Chinese in Guangdong Province, going back to where they were born or where their parents came from, will not necessarily behave in a culturally sensitive way. It's not surprising—they were not exposed to the Cultural Revolution or to the closing of China to the outside world. Meanwhile, they're mostly still trying to distance themselves.

Staff threatened with demotion or loss of their job for whatever reason have been known to threaten blackmail in order to strengthen their case and to make their bosses hesitate to implement their decision. Western expats (and overseas Chinese, though possibly to a lesser extent) can be easily intimidated by such threats. Try to avoid such situations arising in the first place by not allowing resentments to develop; it may be necessary to implement security measures to ensure strict confidentiality of information in order to prevent any potentially damaging information being used against you by a disgruntled employee or even business partner.

Locals will always feel that they have the potential to exercise power over a Westerner or an overseas Chinese because of their local knowledge and *guanxi*. Threats like 'I am a local PRC national', 'I know China', 'I have important friends', and 'I can make trouble for you' are not uncommon. If they know nothing or very little about your most sensitive and private business dealings, you'll feel much more comfortable in the knowledge that these threats are idle and unlikely to do harm, although it's impossible to safeguard yourself totally.

Paying a fair wage

Johnny Ho set up his first office in Shanghai in the spring of 1995, buying the furniture and recruiting the staff—building the company up from scratch. 'The best way to treat local staff here is to give them the feeling that they have a future in the company,' he says. 'An important part of this is that you should pay them generously. Shanghai people are smart—they know that loyalty can't be built from Day One. You need to make a commitment and gain their loyalty by being a generous boss. So I pay my staff 10–15 per cent higher than the market rate.'

Pay is something you shouldn't be mean with. One of the first problems Thu Ho encountered in the joint venture in which she worked was the rapid turnover of staff, who were dissatisfied by the inconvenience of travelling to distant Minhang on the outskirts of Shanghai. They were frequently snapped up by newly opened competitors such as Johnson & Johnson and Bristol Myers Squibb. 'Our salaries were not sufficiently competitive,' Ho reflects. 'We raised our salaries to the market rates—we had to do quite a lot of informal research to find out what others were paying—and now our work-force is quite stable with turnover down to round 10 per cent.'

Another important move by the management was to introduce a five-day working week, long before the PRC authorities actually instituted it across the country. The company also gives all staff free meals while they are at work and has organized annual outings for the whole company, such as a week-long holiday in the beautiful Yellow Mountains District, entirely free of charge. These four new human resources policies, encompassing pay, hours of work, free meals and holidays, have helped make Shanghai RAAS's staff retention rate one of the best of the major pharmaceutical joint ventures in China. The company now has around 290 permanent staff, plus 30 temporary workers.

When Lee Swee Chee set up his team in Shanghai, he followed head office procedure 'to hire the very best people we could get, pay them a little bit more than the market rate, and be very thorough in our selection policy'. Lee wanted to make an upfront statement that he expected a lot from people in return for his investment.

Many executives in China believe that it pays to pay well, because money really is the only motivator. One such executive is **Alan Chieng**. 'Money can solve any problem for the local people —they really believe this. If you give them a good income, you will get good performance out of them. Training can make an impact on their performance, but really money is the strongest motivator.'

Even if it's not necessary to pay extra-high salaries to attract people, it is certainly necessary to avoid paying extra-low salaries. When people know what their friends who work for other companies are being paid for similar work, it's hard to keep them—they feel they are not getting what they deserve. Although money is not the only motivator, lack of money is certainly a strong demotivator.

Know what incentives will work
Johnny Ho confirms, as do people who work for other multinationals, that there is no iron rice bowl at his company—there's no such thing as jobs for life. If most of the

staff members are quite young, they don't really expect it. 'I pay them well and I pay them upfront, but nothing is guaranteed. They must perform,' says Ho. 'If people are lazy, I have to get rid of them, but they will never admit it was because of this reason. I'll give them another chance, but not for long.'

As far as Thu Ho is concerned, the payment or non-payment of bonuses are the only things that really work to ensure a high standard of quality. In pharmaceuticals, even more than for other products, quality is essential—even a matter of life or death, especially in the blood products area. As required by good manufacturing practice, the quality assurance and quality control staff report directly to Ho herself. 'The workers hate these staff, but they are absolutely necessary. We have started a system of incentives and punishments, ie, more or less cash for them based on the achievement or non-achievement of quality. If there are no rejects, they get a bonus. If there's a production shortfall due to rejects, they lose their bonus and the incentive fund for the whole company is reduced. We've tried to show people that if their work is poor, the whole company and all their colleagues suffer. We also encourage them to see the real dangers of low quality in affecting the health of the patients receiving the gamma globulin, albumin and other blood products we manufacture.'

Payments to staff to reward extra-hard work and outstanding achievement don't necessarily need to be in cash. Outings to tenpin bowling arcades, now increasingly popular in many Chinese cities, can be highly popular, as well as banquets and visits to exciting new restaurants, Western as well as Chinese. A trip to the Hard Rock Cafe in Beijing or Shanghai goes down particularly well. You have to bear in mind how the staff will tell their friends about it. 'I did a really good job on the sales of the new product, so my boss, a *laowei*, took me to the Hard Rock Cafe for dinner. It was around RMB 250 per person!' Note the boss actually gave up his or her time to go, and the high cost involved. It may seem rude to reveal the cost of entertainment to a guest in the West, where bills are usually settled discreetly, but in China the full amount of the *maidan* is loudly announced to all and sundry when it comes. Chinese staff can appreciate this kind of non-monetary bonus even more than cash.

Research wage parity

What do you do when a staff member tells you that their friend in General Motors (or whatever company) earns twice as much as they do and, please, can they have a pay rise? If the question is presented in a demanding and aggressive way, some China managers respond by telling the person concerned that they would be well advised to go and join General Motors. However, in the case of staff members who appear genuinely concerned that their labours are not being adequately rewarded and who may, as a result, be feeling a lack of motivation, a similarly concerned attitude should be shown in response. What exactly is their friend's job? Maybe it's more senior, maybe they have more responsibility, maybe they have been longer with the company. Other benefits such as housing, medical and training may not be so comprehensive; it may turn out that when all the benefits are taken into account, the salaries being compared are closer than they at first appear.

Some managers give in and award pay rises on the spot, fearing that they may lose a valued staff member who could be hard to replace. This is not a recommended solution, as the staff member concerned may press further demands. On the other hand, it would also be wrong to make an outright refusal to consider such a request. It is advisable to conduct your own research on salary levels; based on the results of this research, it may be that you do make an increase at the appropriate time. However, salary information, like many other kinds of information, can be hard to come by in China, and depends as much on your own initiative as on any published materials.

One hotel general manager, when pondering this question, said, 'If a staff member asked me why he wasn't paid as much as a friend in a different hotel, I'd ask him "Then why aren't you there instead of here?" If we know someone's seriously underpaid, we would try to make it up, but when we hear these kind of comments it really depends on how it's being asked. Is it a complaint or a suggestion? If it's the latter, we want to hear—we use salary surveys as much as possible, but there are still things which take me by surprise. If we were paying much less than the market rate in Guangzhou, then we'd have higher staff turnover.'

Bench-mark your pay scales
Although you will hear informal tip-offs together with requests for pay rises, serious bench-marking for salaries is in its early days in China. Other foreigners are unlikely to refuse a request to 'Show me yours and I'll show you mine', because everyone is in a similar state of ignorance. Discussions at meetings at chambers of commerce can produce useful information for informal bench-marking,

especially where the chambers in question have set up human resources or related committees. Some of these bodies are now trading this information in news groups on the Internet, although access to cyberspace is somewhat more restricted than elsewhere. Seminars on the subject, often held by salary survey companies, can be as useful for the informal discussions between participants as for the survey material itself. Headhunters can be another source, but watch the level they're working at.

Craig Pepples considers that managers concerned with salary levels should not forget to bench-mark against similar companies, not against State-owned enterprises, for example. 'Remember that, although an SOE manager may seem to be receiving very low pay at around RMB 400 a month, he or she receives many benefits and bonuses. Almost everything is paid for: their salary is just pocket money. They get free housing, meals, medical attention, education for their children, etc.'

A possible second scenario in the context of salaries in China is that of a Hong Kong or Taiwan company which sets up in China, runs the business out of a briefcase, goes around paying into government slush funds, and employs just a few people at high salaries but with no stability or security. Their investment may not be long term—they may decide it's too much trouble, or they can't make profits soon enough. People working for such a company may be well-paid, but they have no long-term future.

The third scenario is the foreign (Western) multinational in China which may or may not pay well. It pays well when pay scales are decided in the United States and there's no-one actually in China who can advise whether the pay is high or low. On the other hand, the pay scales may be relatively low where the company considers that it offers exceptionally high status and learning opportunities; in such cases, it should be able to retain staff for these reasons, rather than because of cash incentives. Many of the companies mentioned earlier as being good at retaining staff are not necessarily high payers.

Craig Pepples suggests that staff wanting highly paid jobs should be warned that 'You don't get anything else but the money'. Other jobs can offer you security over the long term and promotion opportunities, as well as more training and self-development opportunities.

Pepples also warns that you must consider salaries in the context of China. Don't compare China salaries with those in Hong Kong, and don't rate people according to their salaries. For example, a salesperson in Shenzhen might be paid RMB 10,000 a month—in Hong Kong, literally just over the border, he'd be getting HK$60,000. Also in Hong Kong, a secretary can earn HK$20,000 a month—is she more valuable than the salesperson earning RMB 10,000? No, it depends on the context, and the salesperson should be compared with others in China. On the question of salaries, comparing like with like is fundamental.

Use salary surveys with caution

Many Asia-wide salary surveys are too general to be of much use to the China-based manager, and their ranges are too wide. Inevitably, when a salary survey is undertaken, companies at the top and bottom ends of the ranges are interviewed. In China, these ranges are too wide to give any meaningful guidelines—the difference between the highest salary and the lowest salary can be more than 100 per cent. The problem of deriving useful information from salary surveys is exacerbated by companies who set their China pay scales overseas; who more frequently than others make allowances for inflation; who hire new staff, mostly by poaching them from other multinationals and paying a premium in the process; and where the survey is not comparing like with like.

Salary surveys provided for specific industries, such as five-star hotels, are more valuable. The more precise the definitions of the jobs being surveyed, the more valuable is the salary information for bench-marking purposes.

Increasingly, chambers of commerce are conducting surveys of their members that are semi-formal ways of assisting in setting bench-marks; if your company is typical and comparable with others, then this can be useful. But the sample sizes in these surveys can be too small to be meaningful. It's a better idea for your chamber of commerce to link up with other similar bodies in order to create a larger pool to sample. It may be necessary to pay consulting fees to a human resources consulting organization to conduct the survey on behalf of the members — at least this cost can be shared.

Promote benefits over cash
How to motivate your staff when you can't pay them any more is a tough call when many China-based staff have become so money-oriented. In such a situation, the expat manager could emphasize the personal interest the

company has in each staff member, and hold out hopes for an improved situation in the future. It's important to share, as far possible, the reasons why the company is unable to pay more at a certain time. If these reasons are positive and the situation only temporary, such as, 'We don't pay our staff so much at the beginning, when they are first hired, but when you've proved yourself and shown that you can do a good job, then we'll be able to give you a raise', then staff motivation should not be lost. If you can emphasize the learning and skill-building opportunities the company offers, as well as the long-term security, these factors can also offset a lack of cash in hand.

Above all, promoting the family spirit (as discussed above), is the best way to keep a relatively underpaid team. If they feel that you really care about them, and you're giving them as many perks and benefits as you can, they're more likely to stay.

Deflect debate on your pay
A situation where you find your local staff comparing their pay with yours should not arise, as local staff should not be in a position to know an expat executive's pay and benefits. Details like this should all be carefully locked up—the human resources department should be extremely discreet in these matters. However, it is usually quite obvious that expats are paid substantially more; with the help of any newspaper or a roadside hoarding, it's not difficult to find out the cost of housing of a certain size in a certain location.

Those expats who are challenged by local staff need to emphasize their wider experience; their *guanxi* at head office, if they are of the same nationality as the company's founder and senior management; their sacrifices in leaving their own country to move to China; the much-increased cost of living for expats; the fact that, for expats, Chinese cities are amongst the most expensive in the world to live in; and the fact that expats have to carry full responsibility—if anything goes wrong, they have to carry the can. Once what an expat really has to do is clearly defined, few locals would want their job—they prefer to sleep at night.

PART TWO

Managing in China: Your Staff

Chapter 3

Communicating

Commercial enterprises tend to be more effective and therefore more successful if their staff know exactly what is expected of them—this is true of enterprises just about anywhere in the world. However, in China you cannot afford for one moment to give your staff the benefit of the doubt and, from the moment you take up your management position, you need to make things very clear. Be sure the rules you make and the guidelines you set are firm, clear and unambiguous. At the same time, let your staff know that you are starting the way you mean to go on and that you expect them to continue to observe the rules. Making rules is important—a disciplined staff means you are more likely to achieve the goals you have set for the business. Always keep your own goals in mind, and always stick to them.

Jim King talks about spelling everything out, making the rules very clear. He says, 'It's not a question of language, even for an executive who doesn't speak Mandarin. It's on the conceptual side. You have to open up and modernize the minds of your staff. They have to know that you're here to make a profit, and they have to work together as a team to achieve this. So the success of your China business is not just a question of building the infrastructure. It will take you just as long to open the minds of your people to the way foreign companies operate. This may sound easy, especially to people who've been in the US for a long time and who are used to being very open-minded, but it may take another generation before most people in China are ready for more open-mindedness.'

Jim goes on to say that many multinationals are seen as very generous, that everything is negotiable and nothing is checked. 'Only a small minority of people are untrustworthy, but you need to have an efficient checking system in your company, especially in anything to do with money. As long as you are fair in your actions, they will be accepted. For example, you need to set guidelines. What is an appropriate amount to spend when buying lunch for a client—RMB 200 or RMB 500? You must make it clear.'

Many new staff will be unfamiliar with the expectations of a Western company, and you can't expect them to have the judgement to know what is acceptable and what is not. If you say to them, 'RMB 50 is the maximum you can spend on your lunch', don't be surprised if they spend RMB 49.50 (when you're thinking, 'They could buy a lunch-box for RMB 5–10').

Staff supervision

Craig Pepples agrees that, when it comes to managing staff in China, even quite miniscule details must be clearly set out and all the steps of a process identified to ensure successful communication. 'You need to give people detailed instructions, even work-flow diagrams, and be very explicit about how things should be done; they must know that this is different from a typical State-owned enterprise. People must be told explicitly. And you, as the expat boss, must be an expert in the processes of the company, and know them minutely, otherwise you'll lose your mandate as the boss. The boss has to tell everyone how to do things. If you don't know the processes, things will go wrong, and your position will weaken. Your job is to work out how things work, and write out long lists for everyone describing exactly how things should be done. These check-lists are a good stress-reducer for your staff, who feel that if they follow the check-list exactly, they can't go wrong. Of course, this is not always the case, but it does help, and it's much better than a more ambiguous situation.

Do not be careless with small things.
A long pole can be brought down by termites at its foot.
Small things that are disregarded
Are often the cause of failures.

CAI GEN TAI (*Roots of Wisdom*) c. 1630

At Swissotel in Beijing, even small jobs are controlled by 'follow-up slips', small pieces of paper including details of all jobs, such as 'repair ballroom chairs', 'shampoo lobby carpet'. After two days, the first trace goes out—why hasn't this job been done? When will it be done? Every day the supervisors go through all the follow-up slips to monitor the progress of every job. 'One big job's follow-up slip is still outstanding after two years, but eventually it will be done,' says **Alan Chieng**. 'No job is too small to risk being overlooked, hence the need for all these trace slips.'

Be objective and impartial

Fairness is a particularly important quality of the China executive. When running your team like a 'family', sometimes it's difficult not to have favourites. But you must be seen to treat everyone the same, and have a reason for everything you do. Try to be impartial in mediating in disputes between staff, even if one is overwhelmingly to blame. Each must be able to preserve 'face' if they are to be able to continue to work together. Encourage your staff to be impartial and to avoid making choices on personal grounds—emphasize the point that making the right decision is important to the company as a whole, and also to the customers. Everything is personal in China, so teaching staff to be objective and impartial, and to choose suppliers on the grounds of quality and price, not just on *guanxi,* is part of your job.

One's conduct in the world
Must be objective and impartial.
Good fortune and happiness
Will then smile on one.

CAI GEN TAI *(Roots of Wisdom)* c. 1630

Insist on discipline

When you want a high level of discipline in your organization, remember that your view of discipline may be culturally biased. You may think that staff sleeping at their desks shows a low level of discipline and, in a Western context, you could be right. But, in China, it may show a lack of discipline *not* to sleep. Chinese students are told they must sleep after lunch. The Chinese emphasis on health dictates that you must have rest, at least eight hours of it every day. So, if you don't get enough rest at home, maybe because of a lack of air-conditioning or heating, you must get it at work, because if you don't you may become ill. Sleeping after lunch for a couple of hours or even more is actually listed as a right in the 'constitution' of China.

You need to spell out what *you* mean by discipline. Hotels in China with large numbers of staff can have difficulties. Alan Chieng says, 'We used to have a lateness problem, but then we started a rule that if you were late three times, you would get fired. Then people started to produce medical certificates to say they were sick, which is very easy to do in China because you can always find a doctor who will sell you a medical certificate. So now any time anyone is late, they forfeit a day off. This works quite well. We also have a rule against sleeping on duty. Once, after breakfast, a waiter hid under the skirting of a table to sleep, and when he woke up he crawled out from under the skirting—right in front of a big audience attending a function! This sleeping on the job, based on a perception that to protect your health you must sleep as much as you can, is quite common in China, and you must have a policy to deal with it.'

Some companies are more concerned than others with discipline; for example, the German company, Quelle. 'I had to train a fairly green work-force,' says their chief representative, Simon Aliband. 'The pool of well-educated and experienced staff in Shanghai is still limited. I need people not just with an international mind-set, but people who can work in a German office environment, where everything is done by the book, with very rigid rules and quite tough discipline. I had to emphasize the company's culture of discipline and rules right from the beginning.'

Be careful that you, as an expat, know the local rules and don't unwittingly discipline staff for what you may perceive as lapses—they may be permissible. For example, it's common in Shanghai for staff to be allowed rest days—at least two a month—over and above the holidays allowed. Then there's a tendency to go to visit the hospital for the slightest ailment, even a small spot on the cheek. Expats should check with their local human resources department to know the exact rules.

Clearly state your objectives
Even if your company has very clear and simple objectives (such as making money), don't assume that your staff will automatically know them. Remember that many enterprises in China have existed for many decades without such an objective! Don't always assume that your staff are on your side, even if you are providing their livelihood. Chinese are more likely to be loyal to other Chinese, even if this attitude runs counter to what their employer wants.

For example, Simon Aliband of Quelle concentrates his efforts on buying from Chinese suppliers and selling to European customers. His job is to satisfy demanding European buyers while being tough with Chinese manufacturers. 'Our customers' interests are paramount, but often I find that my staff side with the Chinese suppliers, making excuses for them, letting them get away with things I wouldn't allow,' he says. 'After all, my staff are Chinese, they're in China, and they don't necessarily have the mentality that the customer comes first and therefore quality comes first. When there's an argument, they will feel bound to take the Chinese side.'

Emphasize honesty and openness
Know what your staff are doing. Get them to report to you in detail and let them know that you can check things out and they can't fool you. Encourage them to discuss their challenges and problems with their colleagues. Some managers even ask their staff to tell them when they are offered kickbacks from suppliers, so that the bounty can be shared by all. But can you be sure that they will tell you? You need a very special relationship with your staff to share these kind of confidences.

Honesty and integrity among your staff can be further encouraged by quoting a story about a statesman of the Ming dynasty, whose honesty was such that there was nothing but a fresh wind where treasures and cash are usually stored.

> *There was a scholar and official named Yu Qian who prided himself in being upright and honest, in contrast with nearly all the other officials of the Ming Court who were corrupt in the extreme. When these other officials went on missions around the Middle Kingdom, they would bring home valuables they had extorted from the people, carried in their sleeves. When Yu Qian returned from an inspection of the province of Henan, he wrote a poem to show his integrity, scorning the silks and valuables brought back by others, declaiming, 'To see the Emperor, I'll carry nothing but a fresh wind in my two sleeves/So that I will be beyond the reproach of other men.'*

'Nothing but a fresh wind in the two sleeves' (Chinese proverb, Dugong Tanzuan)

Delegate to your staff

Since it appears to be so difficult to delegate, so hard to explain what needs to be done and so unlikely that one will get the results one wants to achieve by delegation, it's easy to be tempted to do everything oneself. This is a big mistake, and the longer it continues, the harder it becomes to delegate anything at all. Finally, when you try to give your staff projects of their own (or monkeys, as they're described in management training jargon), they simply find some way of giving them back to you.

Make it clear that you are delegating by asking your staff to produce their own action plans. Put the ball firmly in their court—tell them you want to know exactly what plans they have, that you will then consider them and make modifications. Always be available to give them help and guidance, and don't leave them entirely on their own, but don't do everything yourself, either. Always set deadlines, or you'll have no idea when anything will get done.

The concerns of your staff

Kathy Bao of Chung Shing took over an existing State-owned department store, overcoming reluctance from many of the staff to join her operation. She understood their concerns—they were worried that they had given up what they saw as a secure job to join an unknown foreign company, another example of the iron rice bowl concept. Bao took a sympathetic but encouraging attitude. 'It took our staff some time to settle down, but after a while they realized that if they performed well, they still had a secure job. Many have since gained promotions, pay rises and have received extensive training,' she says.

At the beginning, when Chung Shing first took over the store, she was aware of a strong 'psychological block', evidenced by feelings of distrust, suspicion and self-protection. This often occurs among local staff whose previous experience has been restricted to the State-owned sector.

'At the start, I tried a combination of rewards and penalties, but the latter didn't work well,' Bao says. 'When they made a mistake, it was better to give them a chance to learn from it, and help them to overcome their inhibitions in communications. They had to first get over this feeling that their "mother store" didn't want them any more. They felt abandoned by former colleagues with whom they had worked for a long time. We had to accept that they had this feeling, and turn them around, and show them that we care, and give them opportunities to improve.' Now, four years later, only one staff member was completely unable to settle in to the new joint venture and had to be made redundant, by mutual consent.

Bao emphasizes the importance of praising people for doing a good job, and building up their sense of pride. 'You need to help them to set goals for themselves and make space for them to improve, but you really have to put yourself in their shoes to do this realistically. There are some really good factories in China and we now have an outstanding retail operation, so it is possible.'

To see the world from the point of view of your staff, you must be very aware of 'face'. The importance of understanding this concept, often perplexing to Westerners, cannot be emphasized too highly in any guide to a China-based career. Among other things, it encompasses not reprimanding staff in front of other staff and praising them publicly; it can also mean sending out messages circuitously.

As **Michael Wu** has found, sometimes the best way to put out a message to an individual is indirectly. You tell other people, and the story spreads around. It may not be efficient or accurate, but it can be face-saving. You must always respect the need for face when disciplining staff.

> *In weeding out scoundrels and flatterers,*
> *It is necessary to leave them a means of escape.*
> *It is like stopping up the hole of a mouse:*
> *When all means of escape have been blocked,*
> *It will chew its way through all your valuables.*
> *In dealing with wrongdoers, one must give them a chance to repent.*

CAI GEN TAI *(Roots of Wisdom)* c. 1630

How miscommunication occurs

'Imagine a seemingly harmless foreigner-to-local conversation,' says **Patrick Un**. 'The foreigner says, "I would like that project plan by next Friday, is that OK?" There are at least three areas of misunderstanding here.'

Time management and planning by individuals are little-understood concepts in a centrally planned economy. Few have any idea of how they fit into a plan, let alone become involved in the planning process. Urgency is another widely misunderstood concept, given China's four millennia of history. For a PRC Chinese to be asked if something is OK would more likely result in puzzlement—of course it's OK, you're the boss! If you were actually understood, to admit that it may not be OK would create a huge loss of face. In China, 'Knowing the spoken language is an advantage,' says Un. 'However, knowing the unspoken language is a definite trump card!'

Many essays and articles have been presented on the subject of miscommunication. Common elements are a failure by the speaker to understand the interests of the listener and vice versa, an avoidance of responsibility on the part of local staff, and the much-discussed aspect of 'face'. Take, for example, three similar true stories, the first from cross-cultural communications specialist, Dr Nandani Lynton.

The setting for this story is the transportation desk of a major international hotel, where a Western business person (WB) is talking with a Chinese employee (CE).

WB   *Do you have cars for airport pick-ups?*
CE   Yes, we have cars.
WB   *I need several cars to pick up incoming visitors tomorrow.*
CE   Yes.
WB   *I need one car to pick up Director X coming in on the 9 o'clock flight from Hong Kong, one car to pick up Mr Y and Mr Z coming in at 12.20 from Bangkok, a seven-seater to pick up a group of six managers coming in at 3.15 from Singapore... Don't you have a pencil?*
CE   I have a pencil.
WB   *Why aren't you writing this down?*
CE   I do not need to write this down.
WB   *Why not?*
CE   Because we have no cars.
WB   *But you told me you have cars.*

CE   But we have no cars tomorrow.

The second story concerns a foreign resident (FR) who wants to move house and phones a company which rents out vans. He asks the staff member there (SM) to help.

FR   *I'm moving house. Do you have a van?*
SM   Yes.
FR   *I need it for Saturday.*
SM   OK.
FR   *How much would it cost?*
SM   The same as the usual rate for a large taxi.
FR   *OK, good. Here's my address (goes into extensive detail on the locations of both the old flat and the new one).*
SM   OK.
FR   *Please arrange for the van to come to my old flat at 2 pm on Saturday.*
SM   But the van is hired out on Saturday afternoon.
FR   *But I said Saturday and you said OK!*
SM   Yes. Saturday morning around 7 am is OK.
FR   *That's too early for me!*
SM   I'm sorry, that's the only time we can make.
FR   *OK, I suppose I could make an early start. Please come at 7 am on Saturday to pick up my furniture and boxes.*
SM   Oh, we can't carry furniture or boxes. The van is for people only—police regulation. Our van is licenced for people only.

The third story concerns a foreign visitor (FV) in a restaurant who orders drinks from a Chinese waitress (CW) for himself and some friends.

FV   *I would like to order four cans of Coke, please.*

CW   If you order one large bottle, it's cheaper than four cans, and will be enough for four people.

FV   *What a good idea! Thank you very much. I'll order one large bottle of Coke. Wow! It's nice to see that customer service has improved so much in China. What a nice waitress!*

CW   Sorry, we don't have any large bottles of Coke.

How did these miscommunications happen? The Chinese did not consider the ultimate aim of the foreigner—in hiring cars, in renting a removal van, in having Cokes to drink—and the foreign person did not consider the 'face' of the Chinese staff. It would have meant loss of face to the Chinese staff to say that they didn't have cars or didn't have a van when they clearly advertise that this is their function. And the waitress was trying to give herself face by appearing to be intelligent and helpful to the visitors, even though her advice was not useful.

A foreigner visiting or living in China who wishes to save time and effort and avoid frustration should try and minimize such miscommunications by focusing on what they want to achieve, remembering that the person they are dealing with, especially in the case of an untrained junior staff member, is unlikely to be doing the same. They will be preoccupied with their 'face' and avoiding any embarrassment to themselves.

Building bridges

Communicating with local staff in China means a lot of emphasis on building trust, and for Jim King this has meant a further adaptation in his management style. 'I have learnt to give opportunities to local staff to prove themselves, and show that they can be trusted and I can have confidence in them. You can't assume there is any trust there until it has been proved. Often, if you give people the chance to succeed, they don't believe you, they think it's propaganda. If this happens, you must first build up confidence. You must play fair between the employees' interests and the company's interests, and especially make the company seem pro-employee.'

Establish trust
Patrick Un advises that the best trust-building strategies are 'to get involved with them, see things from their side, understand their recent history, understand their values and needs'. As we have discussed, the discrepancies between the salaries of expats and locals can cause resentment, tension and mistrust, so, 'as a foreigner, you must quickly show you bring value to them, from your experience, skills, contacts, education and wider exposure.'

As **Lee Swee Chee** points out, 'Local Chinese are not brought up to trust easily. Look at what happened in the Cultural Revolution, which destroyed any sense of trust. They need a strong leader to develop trust. This person must be able to overcome office politics and encourage team spirit by creating glory for the team, not for any individuals. If you promote any one individual, they can become too self-important, and then they feel they can get away with anything. And at all times the manager must be fair, dealing with each issue rather than a person.'

'I spend a lot of time and effort taking care of my local staff, communicating with them, listening to them, and training them,' says **Dan Shao**, a graduate of the famous Dale Carnegie training courses. 'Living in China and working with local staff is painful and time-consuming, but it's worth it. Having spent time team-building, having developed trust, having already made a lot of mistakes, it's now much easier to give them more responsibility, but there's still a long way to go.'

What does Shao feel when his staff leave him and join another company, despite his team-building and training? 'I used to get mad, then I said to myself that I'm generally doing good to society this way, that maybe my influence will last and help other companies and the whole economy, and all of us will benefit in the end. The training we're doing is not just about how to use cosmetics. It's all about image and style, and this must also be good in the long term.'

Encourage loyalty

For some expat executives in China, making staff loyal to you is a first step, then you can encourage them to be loyal to the company. 'When I arrived in Shanghai, the most important thing was that I made the staff loyal to me personally,' says **Mark Gau**. 'It's all very personal. I felt that once my staff were personally committed to me, and that they knew that I respected them, it would be the starting point for building a successful team here, and loyalty to the joint venture.'

This is not such a difficult task with new hires, but it was a real challenge with the 'promotion ladies', women who mostly don't work directly for the joint venture but for the shop or department store which sells the joint venture's products. 'If you show personal respect particularly to these ladies, it goes a long way,' Gau says. 'They don't always expect it. It helps to build their self-esteem. Then we could start training them in being more effective in selling our products, not only in their sales techniques but in their personal appearance. Many of them were old and scruffy and didn't even wear our pantihose, or any pantihose at all. We taught them how to wear make-up and be more glamorous, but it was important that we showed them respect first. This respect is also a key factor in staff retention, now that mobility is high, especially in this sector.'

One potential drawback here will occur if an expat executive is in any way at odds with the company for whom he or she works. Certain members of staff may perceive that their boss, to whom they feel loyalty, has not been treated well by the company, and take sides. In such a situation, it can be difficult for the company when that executive leaves, and the staff members are introduced to a new boss. The new boss has to start all over again, with possibly a negative situation to overcome. If an operation is being localized and an expat executive is replaced, senior management must anticipate the situation by building up a base of loyalty among these staff.

Build harmony within the team
Lee Swee Chee encourages staff members who have a grievance against another, to the extent that harmony within the team is under threat, to justify their complaints in terms of the needs of the business. If there's a complaint against a manager, Lee will discuss it with the person concerned, particularly to find out the reason for the com-

plaint and to establish that it is indeed job-related, and not due to personal feelings. All managers have to rise above office politics and personal clashes to be in line for promotion, Lee maintains. If the complaint concerns a situation which is resulting in poor service to the customer, then it's valid. If it's just a personal grudge, it's not.

Lee keeps an open-door policy towards disgruntled staff. 'What often happens is A complains about B, then C comes in and complains about both of them, so I leave them in an office together to sort it out among themselves,' he says. 'If that doesn't work, then I give them their own territory, their own job function distinct from that of the other person, so they are not stepping on each other's toes any more. The bigger your operation, the easier it is to do this.'

The harmony of the team is very important in China, and staff can easily lose their motivation if they don't feel comfortable within their group. Anyone who disrupts this harmony, but who is nevertheless a talented member of staff you wish to keep, should be removed from the problem area, even sent to another office or branch. But watch for more problems in the future!

Join in social occasions
It is a good move to use social occasions and gift-giving to improve communications with your staff and to continue team-building. **Johnny Ho** has started a program in his company whereby all the company's supervisors visit all their subordinates' families at least once a year. 'Each supervisor has four of five salesmen reporting to him, for example. And he must visit their homes and eat dinner

with the family. It works very well, it helps to bond them together.'

Craig Pepples considers that social functions with your team '...can show you as a human being to your staff, and show your sense of personal commitment in giving up your own time, aside from the value of building personal relationships'. However, he warns that you must also keep your distance. 'You're showing your sense of commitment and you're showing that you care, but you're doing this is in your capacity as general manager of the company; as a human being, you keep some personal distance.' This personal distance is not in the sense of looking down on the staff, but in the sense of preserving discipline and preserving respect to your position.

'It's easy to get some distorted judgement here,' Pepples says. 'Your caring for a person must be in the right proportions; you can't let your personal feelings get involved. People in China expect a certain Confucian manner, a certain "superior person" and "gentlemanly" type of conduct. If you also try to be a friend and colleague on an equal footing, they get confused. The staff have to see you clearly. You should establish human relationships, show that you care, but also show that you're the boss.'

Many local staff in China tend to tell their boss what they think their boss wants to hear—rather than what they may actually think to be true—because they don't want to say 'the wrong thing', and they're not quite sure what 'the wrong thing' or 'the right thing' is. They want to please their boss rather than be truthful to themselves. This way of thinking is not surprising, given that China has a history of testing loyalty and faithfulness by swearing that black is white and white is black, or by calling a stag a horse, or whatever the leader wanted.

Zhao Gao, a eunuch in the Qin court, wanted to usurp power but was afraid that the ministers might not support him. So he used the test of calling a stag a horse. He offered the stag to the Emperor, saying, 'Your majesty, here is a horse I would like to offer to you'. The Emperor replied, 'But, Prime Minister, you've called a stag a horse!' Then Zhao Gao turned to the other ministers and asked them one by one if it was indeed a horse or a stag. Some, anxious to please Zhao Gao, affirmed that it was a horse; others remained silent; others asserted that it was a stag. Then Zhao Gao made his judgement on each: those who called it a horse were promoted, those who were silent were treated with suspicion, and those who called it a stag were executed.

'Call a stag a horse' (Chinese proverb, Shi Ji)

Chapter 4

Training

When attacking someone's faults, do not be too severe
You need to consider how well he will weather what he hears,
When teaching someone by showing him what is good,
Do not pass certain heights, but hit upon what he should be able to follow.

CAI GEN TAI (*Roots of Wisdom*) c. 1630

Craig Pepples has no doubt about the basic role of the expat in China. He says, 'The reason why we as expatriates are in China is to train our staff. We are too expensive to be here just to do a job. Our task is to replicate ourselves, 10 times, 20 times, 30 times over. And we have to make clones who are better than we are, who will inevitably be more culturally sensitive and who will be more committed to China in the long term. We are just here to find successors, many of them.'

Michael Wu also devotes a large proportion of his time to training. Training is given '...in every area you can think of—customer service, courtesy, work skills, English language skills, supervisory skills. And we never stop, not just because of staff turnover, but because you need constant reinforcement.'

Train in the basics first

Craig Pepples found that it is essential to start with basic training and staff orientation, especially if staff have never worked for a multinational company before. 'At first, I needed to spend a lot of energy on what I call "attitude training", getting people into the mind-set of working in a foreign company, giving them a grounding in what is expected of staff in a foreign company, how they should communicate, how I should communicate with them. We did this training quite well, but our staff turnover rate was so high in the beginning that many of the people who received this training have now gone. It's important to keep up the basic training and orientation with all new staff, even though there's a tendency to forget to do this once the office is up and running.'

Pepples also points out the need to insist upon the practical application of material used in the training—that the purpose of training is to become more effective at your job, not just to gain more knowledge for the sake of it. This concept can be at odds with the academic type of education your staff probably received in the past.

> *To know words and to study Zen is book learning.*
> *It is merely building up knowledge of Zen.*
> *He who has not recited a single gatha,*

But who possesses the taste of Zen,
Is awake to the mysteries of its teachings.

CAI GEN TAI (*Roots of Wisdom*) c. 1630

It did not take long for Pepples to learn what local staff find difficult to understand. For example, he asked a newly hired office manager to interview the department heads to find out what they wanted in terms of office supplies and equipment. He suggested she prepare a detailed questionnaire in order to structure the interviews.

However, she thought that this was unnecessary, that people would just tell her what they wanted. This is a common occurrence—there is often no structure or format in the way local staff plan and think. They don't see the point of check-lists and guidelines, which represent structured planning and thinking. The job of the expat manager is to make local staff understand how important these things are in order to maintain standards of quality in all operations.

Alan Chieng worked in the third foreign-managed hotel to be established in Beijing, the China World, and found that the staff were unbelievably inexperienced. 'Most of them had never been in a hotel before, when they first arrived. I was shocked. They had all been to hotel school, but they had just learned in the class-room, from textbooks! They didn't even know about the different departments needed to run a typical hotel. The local hotel schools in China have no overseas teachers and, until recently, there were no overseas-managed hotels in China. So when I was training staff at the China World, I had to start from scratch, teaching them in how to deal with guests, everything. It was extremely basic.'

Chieng's approach to training, influenced by this need to go back to basics, is very practical. 'In setting up a table for dinner, for example, I will show them where everything goes, measure the space between the plate and knives and forks with a ruler, and write down all the measurements. I then take a photo of this set-up and give it to them for reference. They have to pass an exam on this. If they fail, they lose their bonus. It's serious stuff.'

Chieng has also focused on making the staff more proactive. It used to be that they would wait for customers to complain before they would do anything. 'Now, for example, they have to set the temperature for each function room, and keep checking it, and be more proactive about making sure everything is in order.'

Building a corporate culture in China

In creating a corporate culture in keeping with the overall culture of the organization world-wide, Craig Pepples feels he was lucky to come in at the beginning, when his company first set up its China operation, and to have the opportunity to hire new staff and build a culture from zero. 'We've created a bubble within China of our own company culture, an island of continuity through having grown our own people, and in keeping with the expectations of our head office. But I sometimes forget about the outside world, and that we must function with the outside world! Building a clear culture took a long process of orientation, despite having the advantage of being able to start from zero and having continuity over the last three years.'

For Pepples's operation, a wholly foreign-owned enterprise, the challenge of creating a corporate culture is quite different from the challenge confronting expatriates who are trying to create such a culture with a joint venture partner, or have taken over an existing factory. Here, the process is much harder. Even when workers want to identify with the foreign partner and see the benefits of the foreign cash and technology inputs, their ability to adopt a new culture is limited. But it can be done—again, it depends on training and continual reinforcement of that training.

When creating a corporate culture throughout several offices in China, there are three possible approaches, all with negative and positive aspects. It's important to be aware of the advantages and disadvantages of all three approaches.

The first approach is to hire local people in each office. They will happily work together as a team and they understand the local context. However, it will need a lot of training before they conform to the head office corporate culture, because there may be no-one (besides the expatriate overall manager) to act as a catalyst in transforming them into this new culture. This process can be likened to the way in which yoghurt can be made by boiling milk and adding a spoonful of an existing yoghurt culture to replicate that yoghurt.

The second approach is to build a China headquarters office and to subsequently open regional offices as satellites of the first; the headquarters office serves as a model and staff are then moved out to the regions. Although it sounds easier, because it's following an existing format, Chinese people are notoriously provincial, and Beijing people would be most unhappy to be expected to work in Shanghai, and vice versa. It's not just a question of their personal tastes and *guanxi*, but it's physically difficult for people to move within China, due to heavy restrictions on housing and school education (which is normally reserved for residents), as well as the *houkou* problem.

The third approach to building corporate culture is to send more Westerners and overseas Chinese, who have experience of working in head office, to each office in China. This approach can ensure a fairly strict adherence to head office rules and increase the likelihood of head office culture being duplicated elsewhere. However, can your company afford so many expats? And what happens when they leave—will the corporate culture go with them?

Weaknesses of PRC staff

Many management topics are not generally taught in Chinese universities nor are their principles practised in Chinese companies, at least, not in the way that they are understood and known in the West, such as human resources management. Also, the way of teaching in Chinese universities has led to what many regard as a further weakness in Chinese staff, that of passivity and a lack of active criticism.

As **Patrick Un** emphasizes, training should encompass both teaching a theory and demonstrating its meaning and application—of vital importance in China, given the lecturing style of the highly theoretical training common in Chinese educational establishments. 'Concepts like good presentation, quality and being customer-oriented are best taught by illustrations, examples and comparisons,' says Un. 'At a recent management training session, the participants were complaining about the hotel facilities. I turned it into a brainstorming and problem-solving exercise about how we would improve these aspects. It saved me the embarrassment of having appeared to have made a bad venue choice, as the participants thought it was an intentional part of the training!' Such participative activities and real-life examples are essential in driving the training message home.

Philip Chen, who has worked in the insurance sector and has for many years been primarily concerned with staff training, feels that even though it's possible to teach local PRC staff to sell, they find it very hard to sell intangible products, like insurance. 'They would rather sell something very tangible, so they can point to it and say, "This is it, and you can buy it, and it costs this much". They find it very difficult to handle customer objections in a way that shows their initiative—all they know is what you've taught them. It's very hard to teach them to think for themselves. They just look up the list of objection-handling arguments that you used to teach them, and if they don't find a particular objection on their list, they don't know what to do, except call their boss.'

Alex Chang finds that the greatest weaknesses of the staff, particularly his sales teams, are in supervision, management and leadership skills. 'In the West, young people would spend two or three years in a basic sales job before being promoted to supervisor. Here in China, you just can't wait that long. I find myself promoting people with only six months' experience. Then, of course, they just don't have any management experience and, not surprisingly, lack the mature judgement of experienced managers.

'And then you have another problem. You can't promote everybody; in any case, after a few years, your company's growth will slow and the opportunities for promotion will be less. Then you will lose people to other companies, for the simple reason that they have suffered loss of face because they weren't promoted and some of the others were. And they still lack management experience, even though they may be good at selling or some other functional area. Many of them just don't realize that management is a skill, not just a position or a sign of status.'

Alan Chieng also finds this problem in the hotel world. 'Waiter turnover is very high, so anyone who does stay is likely to be promoted. There's such a shortage of skills that very early on waiters can be promoted to captains. In Singapore, you would have to be a waiter for three to five years before you could be promoted to captain, but here we have captains aged 17 with only six months' experience.

'It's no wonder we have customer service problems—all the hotels do. It's impossible to expect the same level of discreet, intelligent customer service and sensitive handling of customer complaints from such junior staff. And when we have good ones, they will inevitably be poached. We can send some of them as local expats from Beijing to other provinces, where they can earn much larger salaries, but your hotel chain must be extensive to be able to do this.'

Objectives of a training program

Be aware of the difference between a training 'needs' analysis and a training 'wants' analysis. If you make a list of possible training course topics and ask your staff to indicate those in which they are interested, you'll get a 'wants' analysis. They want to study the Internet, marketing and advanced English; however, they actually *need* to study accounting, sales and basic English. The Internet is very fashionable in China—you can walk down any main street of a major city in China and see a young man with a wooden box giving out leaflets, all in Chinese, with one word in English, in large bold letters: INTERNET. But will it be useful for your staff to study the Internet? In some cases, 'yes'; in many cases, 'no'—not all of the Internet, anyway. Similarly, marketing is upmarket and trendy, where sales is low-class. To admit you may need basic English could lead to a distinct loss of face; better to ask for advanced English, even if you're not sure what's going on during the class. You can always sit at the back of the class-room and catch up on that sleep you need.

Train to improve quality
Kathy Bao concentrates her training efforts on improving quality. 'You just can't expect people to produce items of

the quality you want. To them, it's good enough. They don't actually see a lot of the defects; they've compromised on quality for so long.' Staff don't bother as much about cleanliness in their working conditions as they might in many other places. Bao finds she must spend a lot of time on basic production training. 'Every week we have to clean the work-tops so that the clothes being made don't get dirty, and the sewing machines must be cleaned every month.'

Training for quality is '...the toughest problem of operating in China,' Bao says. 'Your staff will think you are too hard on them and that you should compromise. But you must understand their standards and encourage them to reach higher.' It's not easy, though; much of the basic infrastructure is still missing. 'If we want the factory to send us a sample and it's raining, we have to wait until tomorrow. Our suppliers can't afford a taxi, the buses are infrequent, and all they have are their bicycles.'

Michael Wu also focuses on training for high standards of quality—and also on maintaining his determination to keep his standards high. It is important to Michael to never tolerate poor quality, otherwise he would start to compromise. 'When I first arrived in China, I made a big effort to improve the quality of service in everything we do here. And I have to keep at it. But when you're here a long time, you tend to get used to substandard quality. This is a real danger—you begin to get used to second-best. When I go away and come back, I really notice the substandard quality again, and become very demanding. In the matter of training your staff to improve quality, it's very important to leave China regularly to get a "reality check", and to stimulate yourself towards further improvements.'

Train to retain staff

'Training is a double-edged sword,' says Patrick Un. 'If you don't train people, they will leave. If you do train them, they'll get head-hunted.' With so many foreign companies in China, there's a huge demand for well-trained staff, and local employees in multinationals are becoming alarmingly mobile. But training is essential in building a competent and even partially loyal work-force, and local staff working in a multinational will come to expect it and value it. It would probably be a mistake to *not* train people for fear of them becoming more attractive to head-hunters or competitors.

'Having delivered training and public seminars to more than a thousand people all over Asia, I find that the Chinese people are the most enthusiastic. Some executives working in China find them slow, but in reality they just lack the exposure. In keeping with the emphasis on education in Chinese culture, they have an insatiable hunger for knowledge and information.'

It would be unwise to deny your staff the opportunity to undergo training. However, to train and retain, you just have to make sure that your staff appreciate your company's commitment to training, and realize that if they went elsewhere they just would not receive so much training of such high quality. A human resources manager with the Danish trading company, EAC, in Beijing described how one of his company's staff members left EAC to join another company, but returned to the fold once he realized that his new company just didn't care so much about training and didn't offer many training opportunities. He had taken it for granted that all companies would be as keen about training as EAC.

Lee Swee Chee uses training as a way of retaining staff, to encourage staff to feel a sense of ownership of their jobs, and to create an American-style corporate culture. 'People won't stay long if they can't make decisions, if they're not doing "real" work, if they're not being helped to grow,' he says. 'When the staff have ownership of their work, they enjoy their work more; then we can introduce new concepts and teach them new skills. We're doing a lot of skill development training, particularly basic management skills, negotiating skills, presentation and communication, even business and personal etiquette training.

'When the whole office has had this kind of training, we can get the staff away from being locals and say to them, "Hey, you're in a US company now!"' And, he says, part of the ethos of being in a US company is to be busy and not sit around reading newspapers.

Instil a sense of responsibility

Empowerment is one of the most needed yet most challenging of all concepts to teach in China, where reluctance to take responsibility is almost legendary. A major European multinational operating in China once had 25 of its managers in a management training class. When asked to choose from a list of motivational factors, most chose the chance to gain 'a sense of achievement', 'recognition and praise' and 'advancement and promotion': only three said they were inspired by the chance to have greater responsibility. It's hard to explain the links, well understood in the West, between authority and responsibility, and authority, responsibility, and a large salary. Basically, expatriates in China are being paid to take responsibility, largely because, in many cases, local staff are not yet ready for it.

Local staff find being given responsibility for a task and being asked to develop their own initiative very daunting, too big a commitment, too dangerous and with only negative connotations. They don't think of the possible rewards, just of the possible awful consequences of making a mistake. To ask a local member of staff to take responsibility can be like asking a tiger for its skin.

A gentleman of the Zhou dynasty wanted a beautiful fur robe from a rare animal, and also had a taste for the delicate-tasting meat of a sacrificial animal. So he went to ask a fox for its skin and a sheep for its flesh. The animals, beckoning to their mates, all fled to the mountains and the forests. For several years, the man was unable to get a fur robe or a sacrificial animal. This story later changed and became known as asking a tiger for its skin.

'Ask a tiger for its skin' (Chinese proverb, Taiping Yulan)

Training to build empowerment and a sense of responsibility can be a combination of class-room and on-the-job training, with the emphasis on role plays that are *real* and where the consequences of not taking responsibility are all too obvious.

Alan Chieng encountered a real problem with lack of empowerment when he first started working in the hotel industry in Beijing. Staff didn't check the function room bookings; they either left it to the expats or just didn't think about it. Once an oversight was discovered, they would go into panic mode and wouldn't know what to do. 'We had a booking from a customer for a cocktail party and dinner, but the staff looking after the functions just forgot about them. They remembered only when the organizers turned up 15 minutes before the event. Then they panicked—they were just going to cancel it. Anyway, all the expats in the hotel dropped everything and rushed down and set up the party and the dinner. As we were late starting, we had to give this function to the customer for free. This would be less likely to happen now, because we've been able to instil a greater sense of empowerment.'

Michael Wu is concerned with training for empowerment, however difficult and time-consuming this might be. 'One of my hardest tasks is promoting initiative and a sense of empowerment amongst my staff,' he says. Encouraging individual decision-making means clear rules need to be set before staff feel comfortable enough to make their own decisions. 'I've told them that if there's a dispute and it's about anything which costs less than RMB 500, it can be waived without asking me. If a customer finds a cockroach in his dinner, for example, the staff member can waive the whole bill. For a while, staff still came to me to sort out a RMB 20 mini-bar bill query. But gradually, with more direction, my staff are making more of their own decisions.'

Training for empowerment and to develop a sense of initiative is one of the biggest challenges faced by an expatriate manager working in China. Scenarios such as the following are only too common. In the first scenario, an expatriate businesswoman (EB) is at her office, talking with the Chinese receptionist (CR) at the reception area, near the fax machine.

EB   *I see there's a fax stuck in the fax machine, and only half of it has come out.*

CR   Yes.

EB   *What's the problem?*

CR   We have run out of fax paper.

EB   *Do we have more fax paper in the store-room?*

CR   Yes.

EB   *Do you know how to put it in the fax machine?*

CR   Yes.

EB   *When did the fax machine run out of paper? Just now?*

CR   About midday. [It is now 4 pm.]

In most cases, the expatriate becomes exasperated, yelling at the receptionist about the hundreds of people who've been trying to send faxes for the last three hours, unable to believe that the receptionist hasn't thought of replacing the fax paper. The receptionist, embarrassed and suffering loss of face, will respond that no-one told her to do it.

A better way of handling the situation is to politely instruct the receptionist to replace the fax paper immediately, and ask questions and make comments along the lines of, 'Do you think anyone's been trying to fax us?', 'What would have happened if anyone tried to fax us?', 'Do you think fax machines have a memory and store faxes that haven't been transmitted?', 'Maybe we should make sure the fax machine always has paper in future. You don't need to ask anyone first', 'Maybe we should write a note and stick it to the fax machine so that everyone will know to put more paper in, even when you're away,' and 'Here, help me write a Chinese translation to my note. Thank you very much!' This second approach is more face-saving for the receptionist, helps her see the downside of not acting herself, and is more likely to lead to a permanent solution.

The second story concerns a Hong Kong businesswoman (HB) who is trying to teach a local salesman (SM) how to overcome customer objections when negotiating the rental of an apartment.

HB *When you're trying to get the customer to rent an apartment, you tell them, for example, that this particular flat costs US$3000 a month, and they have to pay a month's rent in advance and a month's rent as our fee.*

SM What if that's too expensive for them?

HB *Then you see if you can find a cheaper flat.*

SM Do they still have to pay the rent in advance and fees?

HB *Of course!*

SM What if they don't want to pay the month's rent in advance?

HB *Then they won't be able to rent the flat!*

SM What if they don't want to pay our fees?

HB *Then we don't do business with them!*

SM What if they don't want to rent a flat at all?

At this point, the businesswoman becomes frustrated. She considers the salesman untrainable, unable to think for himself and possessed of no sense of initiative or imagination. If she had known it, she would have taken into account the fact that many people in China have no experience of selling and are worried about making mistakes if they are given responsibility. So they'll want to know the correct response for every possible outcome they can think of, however obvious the answer may appear. The businesswoman could have praised the salesman for asking questions, but could have encouraged him to develop more initiative by answering his own questions, by asking him, 'What do you think?'.

The third story concerns a Taiwan manager (TM), who is inspecting a delivery of bottles of shampoo at a client's shop while speaking to a local factory packer (FP) over the telephone.

TM   *Did you pack that consignment of four boxes of 12 bottles of shampoo XYZ brand to client ABC's shop yesterday?*

FP   Yes.

TM   *Did you know that the bottles had no tops on them?*

FP   Yes.

TM   *Why did they have no tops on them?*

FP   The person who puts the tops on the bottles was off sick yesterday.

TM   *So why didn't you put the tops on?*

FP   Not my job.

The Taiwan manager is likely to scream at the packer for doing a poor job, whereas the packer just did the job he's paid to do, without asking questions and without causing any trouble. The manager's approach would be more effective if he could make the packer understand the disaster he caused—shampoo leaking through the boxes all over the customer's shop floor—and the resulting problems for the company, such as loss of reputation and the need to repeat the order free of charge. Quality inspection in China is often seen as the job of a particular quality inspection officer, and no-one wants to take the initiative to do his job if he's not there. Training staff to care about quality and to be prepared to take the initiative to put right a quality problem is a big challenge, and can't be achieved overnight. Since staff in China often don't want to get a fellow worker into trouble, they are likely to avoid mentioning even a serious quality problem.

Teach new concepts

What if your training efforts are directed in particular at changing the Chinese corporate culture to an American or European corporate culture at your joint venture or wholly foreign-owned company? What if, for example, you want to change the emphasis of the company from being production-oriented to being marketing-oriented?

'When we acquired our China business, it was very product-driven,' says an executive in Shanghai. 'The production people ran the show. In the beginning, for instance, all pricing was cost-based; the salespeople had no involvement. Now we're providing them with a different kind of leadership. They are recognizing the need for marketing, but their interpretation of implementation is still different sometimes.

'For example, we tried to encourage consumption of our products through a special promotion which gave the customers a free product for every two they bought. The local salespeople didn't see it that way—they wanted the free product to be packaged separately, and given as a free gift. This wasn't the idea. My concern was to increase the amount of consumption; theirs was to stop the sales staff from stealing the extra products, which they thought would happen if we didn't track the free ones more carefully by giving them different packaging.'

It was also a challenge for this executive to show the salespeople that customers associate the product with the person who is selling it. If that person is unattractive and unsophisticated, the products will be seen that way, and customers will not be interested in the product, unless it's exceptionally low-priced. 'I had to teach them how brands die, and to show the relationship between a brand and customer service, and the overall success of the business, and why it's good to appear to be an international brand, supported by a famous international brand name,' he says. 'But, in explaining this, I find it very important to not issue orders but explain why something is important.'

Offer job rotation and encourage 'big picture' thinking

*Performing great achievements
But giving no thought to the seeds of virtue for the future:
This is but flowers blooming
And withering before the eyes.*

CAI GEN TAI (*Roots of Wisdom*) c. 1630

It's important to encourage staff to understand the wealth of possibilities open to them if they are successful in their jobs; telling stories about particularly successful employees can help in this regard. Offering job rotation is a good way of giving people a new job as well as encouraging them to stay with the company. If they feel the need for a change, you can still keep them, but with new challenges. However, you need to have a big operation in China to be able to do this successfully. One good example is Holiday Inn.

'We are more daring than most,' says Michael Wu, of Holiday Inn Guangzhou. 'My former secretary is now the executive in charge of housekeeping. This was a potentially risky move, as she's facing new kinds of pressure, and she's not yet sure about herself in this role. But the guests and her colleagues think she's doing great.'

Craig Pepples also tries job rotation on an informal basis, including his secretary, too. 'This job now has a reputation as a stepping-stone for more senior and challenging opportunities,' he says. His former secretaries have gone on to senior positions in marketing and sales.

In Pepples's company, managers needing to hire more staff are encouraged to seek them internally. Of particular note is one promising staff member who has gone from sales to advertising copy-writing to seminar organizing. So training to develop staff members' full capabilities, rather than training them for specific jobs, can encourage retention; job rotation becomes a possibility, a better alternative that having them leave to find a job in another company.

Staff can be highly motivated by not just the training provided by international companies but the opportunity to travel in their jobs, and in some companies and industries this is possible. Take Holiday Inn, for example—not only do they offer job rotation, but geographical rotation. Not only Westerners and overseas Chinese can be expatriates; local Chinese can also find themselves in distant regions when the hotel sends experienced hotel department managers from Beijing to more distant properties, such as in

Urumuqi. Such transfers don't always work, particularly in places where local dialects are widely used and there's some animosity to people from other parts of China, such as in the case of Shanghai and Guangzhou.

Alan Chieng explains that many staff in China tend to see only their department and think about their job in a very limited context. 'For example, the bellboys working at the front door tend to think that they are there only for room guests, to carry their luggage. If we have a function, and the organizers are arriving with boxes, they hesitate about whether they should help them. I hear from our customers that some hotels are worse—that if they're not room guests, they're like second-class citizens and have to carry all their things by themselves and use the back door.'

This problem of thinking only about one's own department can make it difficult for an organization to provide a seamless, unified service to customers. Staff must understand that it's a customer's overall, total experience that counts. It's no good having a great sales team and poor order fulfilment. It's no good having great products without maintenance support. It's no good having great waitress service with poor food. Job rotation can help with this problem, as can regular reviews of customer complaints.

The only way to change this narrow focus is to train them to see their work in a wider context, to make them understand what effect the tasks they do have on other parts of the organization and to take responsibility for the overall results and not just their small area of activity. Many local staff tend to behave like blind men sizing up an elephant—they make a judgement based on only their narrow focus of interest without thinking about the whole.

A king asked for an elephant to be brought to him, together with six blind men, who he instructed to touch the elephant one by one and say what they thought it was. The first, who touched the elephant's tusk, said it was like a turnip; the second, who touched the elephant's ear, said it was a dustpan; the third, who touched the foot, said it was a pestle; the fourth, who touched the elephant's back, thought it was a bed; the fifth felt its belly, and said it was a jar; and the last blind man, who touched the elephant's tail, thought it was a rope.

'Blind men sizing up an elephant' (Chinese proverb, Daban Niepan Jing)

Encourage results-oriented attitudes

Staff in China must be encouraged to bear in mind the results of their work and realize that they help to achieve an ultimate objective. They should be encouraged to celebrate outstanding sales results and should share in the concern over poor sales results, for example. Local staff should be deeply involved in analysing the reasons for both, since the customers are local, too. Their input is especially valuable for the expat manager, especially if he or she is a Westerner.

Local staff should also be involved in long-term strategic planning: 'What can we do to lock in our customers and increase our repeat business rate?', 'How can we improve the quality of our promotional material?', 'What can we do to attract customers to this product, as it doesn't seem to be very popular right now?' Local staff can help immeasurably with these questions, and gain a results-oriented attitude in the process.

Open their minds

The spacious of mind considers a tiny room
As expansive as Heaven and Earth.
You are what you think.
If your mind is expansive,
Then it has no limits with regard to things.
Such a mind abides everywhere.

CAI GEN TAI (*Roots of Wisdom*) c. 1630

Using practical exercises and participative role-plays in training certainly helps to open minds and widen horizons, if only because it's a different form of training than the conventional Chinese university style. Training which gives local people the opportunity to take part in a simulated exercise can be quite mind-blowing, but it needs a lot of debriefing and follow-up when the principles of the training are applied in a work situation, otherwise it might be seen as just a game.

Yet all training should aim at mind-opening. It can be used to overcome any perceived resistance to strangeness and things foreign; for example, objections such as, 'This is not relevant to China...this will never work in China'. Such objections have lessened over the last few years, but beware of those whose minds open slightly for a few moments then close again, like a clam.

To make a success of mind-opening training, you, as the expat boss, should conduct the training yourself, little and often. Keep reviewing what your staff have learned from this training and what has been implemented as a result. You should promote training as a reward, not as an entitlement; it's not a bonus, it must be earned and actively used.

You should also carefully seek feedback on the results of external training courses on which your staff have been sent. How useful were these courses? At all costs, try to prevent your staff viewing external training courses as opportunities to take a break from work or to look for a new job. As discussed earlier, training can be a double-edged sword.

Training to retain: a case study

The Shanghai office of the famous oil company, Shell, has grown to nearly 100 staff since it re-entered the China market in the late 1980s. As mentioned in Chapter 2, this company enjoys a remarkable level of staff retention, which is seen as closely related to its emphasis on training. Shell has lost only eight people in the last three years; of these, most left because of spouse relocation, not because of any dissatisfaction with the company. The only staff member who left to join a competitor rejoined Shell three months later, bringing two of the competitor's best staff with him! Not surprisingly, this is a favourite story of former general manager for the East China region, Nick Pennington, since relocated to Shell London but still remembered fondly by Shell staff. There's a lot of respect for senior managers, a strong team spirit and a keen sense of the history and culture of the company. This is no accident—it's part of the plan.

Shell's management and executive-level training has a relatively structured approach, and benefits from a diversity of styles and formats. General Affairs Manager, Jason

Su, and Training Manager, Cindy Yang, both local Shang-hainese, present courses themselves; other Shell trainers and outside providers run other courses. Thus Shell China provide their staff with three different perspectives on training.

The first tier of Shell's training, taught by local Shell staff, was brought in from Europe and localized for Chinese consumption. Entitled 'Front Line Leadership', it covers the basic skills of interpersonal and problem-solving effectiveness, and change management. These courses are taken by specified levels of staff across Shell world-wide. The second tier includes courses taught by outside suppliers, such as in time management and presentation skills. The third tier courses are taught by Shell trainers at the regional training centre in Singapore, and include week-long programs called 'Managing Self' and 'Managing People'. These are a big investment for Shell, as each person must be flown there and accommodated.

The balance between the three approaches to training works well, according to Jason Su. 'If we did all the training ourselves, we wouldn't have too many new ideas coming in. But if we used outside trainers, we wouldn't get such an opportunity to build the Shell culture. And we couldn't afford to send everyone to Singapore. Those courses are more for senior managers at the moment.'

Shell's training is also only for staff who've already proved their mettle and have been with the company for over a year. The selection process for Shell staff is a very careful one, and based around the development of fresh graduates rather than hiring from other companies. 'If we had to choose between two job candidates—one with 10 years' selling experience but with poor English and a non-graduate, and one who's a fresh graduate, inexperienced, but with good English, and who is bright and ambitious —we would always choose the second,' says Jason Su. 'We focus on the future, and long-term staff development.'

Shell also practice a carefully managed system of job rotation whereby every three years staff are trained in and moved to new positions. Su was originally Training Manager before his step up to General Affairs Manager. This kind of career management of staff and manpower planning is fairly unusual in China. Ironically, it's not done because people don't stay, but one of the reasons people leave is because they're not sure where they're going in the future.

Shell's number of training days is an impressive 15–20 per staff member, for management and executive-level training alone. There's also a big commitment to technical training: Shell staff in Beijing led their staff through an intensive six-week course on liquid petroleum gas handling and distribution. Without including the technical and industry-specific training, the annual training cost to Shell is up to US$200,000 per hundred staff members. In terms of savings on recruitment, getting staff up to speed and achieving a strong corporate culture, the Shell executives heading up the China operation consider this kind of expenditure well worth it. 'We have given up calling people in Shell,' confided a Shanghai-based head-hunter. 'They are very well-trained, smart, have great English language skills, are hard-working and reliable. Our clients would love to have them. But we can never get them out.'

Chapter 5

Internal politics and staff expectations

Craig Pepples finds that internal politics is an inevitable aspect of life in an office or factory in the PRC. He says, 'You can find out a lot about how people relate to what's going on, and it's good to be aware of the nature of the internal politics of your organization. At different points, staff will want to sit down and talk about the power structure of the company, the boss, and how they're getting on in the company. There's a tradition in China of doing this; in the past, when everyone was in a State-owned enterprise, they had plenty of time to sit around discussing all the power struggles going on. If you, as the expatriate boss, get involved in these conversations, you can get anxious. Sometimes it can be an advantage not to speak their language and therefore not to get so involved!

But it's necessary to acknowledge that they are thinking about this, and that they're concerned about their role in the organization.'

Pepples has also discovered that many China staff have an attitude that 'Our time has come!' He says, 'After years of suffering during the Cultural Revolution and years of poverty, hardship and no clear future prospects while China was closed to the outside world, many young people in China think the world owes them a bright future now, that they are the promised generation.' While this is true for many, and undoubtedly the opportunities in China are now greater than ever before, not everyone will reach the promised land. Many will be disappointed and all will have to learn an often painful lesson that opportunities have to be earned.

Coping with internal politics

Pepples has gradually developed a rather relaxed strategy as far as office politics are concerned. He says, 'You should give each one an understanding of your commitment to them and concern for them, and then say to yourself that all this internal politics chit-chat doesn't matter. In China, people regard themselves as having plenty of time for gabbing, much more so than in the Western context. You should let them do it from time to time, and filter out anything you can learn from it. I learned a painful lesson, of spending hours and hours worrying what my staff were thinking about, but now I realize that they're just gabbing.'

Identify cliques that may be dangerous

All offices in China develop cliques: some are formed of members of the same department, some went to the same school or university, some come from the same town or city in China. Beijing people working in Shanghai and vice versa will certainly hang out in a clique together, sharing their mutual scorn of people from the other city. Sometimes these cliques are harmless and just social groups who go out arm-in-arm at lunch-time together.

However, sometimes cliques can be dangerous and cause bottlenecks in projects and disruption in communications. The people responsible are just looking after themselves with no thought of the damage they are doing to the company. Either the results of what they're doing must be brought to their attention and their behaviour stopped, or the clique must be split up and its members moved within the office. The more staff members focus on the overall objectives of the company and the more they feel like a team in harmony with the rest of the company, the less likely they will be to want to form a damaging clique.

Leo Yang, an overseas Chinese from Taiwan who manages the San Marlo ice-cream factory in Shanghai's Pudong district, faced the problem of managing local Shanghai staff, customers and suppliers who would form a clique and speak in the Shanghainese dialect during board meetings with himself and fellow Taiwan colleagues. These private asides were leading to mistrust and annoyance. So the Taiwan people gave them a taste of their own medicine, speaking in the Taiwan dialect. It was then promptly agreed that Mandarin only should be used during these meetings. 'And this really worked! We've not had the problem again,' says Yang.

Watch for hidden agendas

In any organization in China, information is power. So the most important jobs are those close to the boss, and close to the information. Those members of staff close to **Thu Ho** and other senior managers in their joint venture in Shanghai jealously guard their positions, so when they were asked to recruit additional staff, they tended to recommend relatively mediocre individuals who were unlikely to threaten their positions and who spoke no English (Ho does not speak fluent Mandarin). 'Many of the staff expect to operate in a top-down culture, with no sharing of information, and where having ideas is seen as dangerous. You cannot attack someone's ideas without attacking that person himself, and revealing your own ideas exposes you too much,' says Ho.

To minimize the possibility of exacerbating the internal politics of the joint venture, Ho looks for certain qualities in her people. 'When hiring, I choose staff who are intelligent and, above all, aggressive and hard-nosed, who stand up for themselves and are strong, and who want to get on with the job.' Politics within the company is encouraged by staff who are weak and insecure. 'When staff are given the responsibility of hiring for your company, insist on what you want. They will find some excuse, saying they can't find a person who speaks English, for example. This is rarely the case. Watch out for hidden agendas.'

Be aware of regional loyalties

As already indicated, loyalty to one's city or region is strong in China, where mobility is still strictly limited by the *houkou* system, and where one's *guanxi* very much depends upon where one lives. If you move to another city in China, you're a fish out of water. So, if you're a PRC Chinese, what do you do? Find other people living there who come from your home town, then, if you have the chance, persuade your boss to hire them.

As we have seen, this is the way cliques form. So, as the boss, you must counteract the possible negative effects of a clique formed as a result of loyalty to a different part of China by encouraging loyalties of a different kind. Encourage loyalty to the company or a department or to a particular product line; ensure that everyone, whether a member of a clique or not, is loyal to the achievement of your goals.

Understanding staff expectations

There are many things an expatriate manager in China should be aware of when it comes to staff relations, and one of them concerns the expectations of PRC staff. Staff joining a multinational company often expect to be offered the opportunity, sooner or later, to go on overseas trips and learn Western business methods. Others, however, view Western companies negatively and are reluctant to leave the perceived safety of a State-owned enterprise. Then there is the prospect of localization—a long-term undertaking.

Be selective with overseas travel

Patrick Un explains why PRC staff join a multinational company. 'In Beijing alone, there are 10,000 foreign-invested enterprises, which are attracting more and more State-owned enterprise employees. They join companies like our own, Unisys, and Siemens and Motorola, for example, especially for the attractive salaries. Their pay becomes a multiple of their previous income, but they lose valuable benefits like subsidized housing. However, for them, joining a foreign company opens a door on the outside world, literally offering them the opportunity to go overseas—in a country where it's extremely difficult to get a passport to travel.'

It's important to bear this in mind when hiring staff who previously worked in a State-owned enterprise—sooner or later they will be asking about when they can go on a trip outside China. **Lee Swee Chee** wants to feel that a team is well-developed and strong in the company before any overseas exposure is possible; only when the members of the team are ready for the passing-on of authority can an overseas trip be contemplated. Overseas trips are not for new, untried or junior staff. Only the most outstanding managers are sent to the United States for training; they are the ones who are receptive to new ideas and want to improve themselves.

Try to make staff feel secure

Kathy Bao says that when her company, Chung Shing, set up the Sunrise Department Store, it essentially took over an existing State-owned local business and many of the staff didn't want to leave and join her. 'This was a very traditional Chinese retailing store,' she says. 'We took over the staff, chose entirely new merchandise, and renovated the building completely. We took over around two-thirds of the staff, around 300 in number, with the remainder moving to the "mother store", the headquarters of the old local operation. Those members of staff we chose for the new Sunrise store were not necessarily glad to be working with us: they felt that they were unwanted cast-offs, that we were not offering them the iron rice bowl that they had enjoyed in the past. They were afraid to leave the State-owned sector and work in a joint venture. We paid them 30 per cent more than their former colleagues, but some were still uncertain if they really wanted to join us.'

You may encounter similar negative perceptions. There is little that can be done apart from offering a good salary, good working conditions and assurances of security of employment. Only time will effect a change of mind-set.

Move slowly towards localization
'Many expatriates would like to promote local staff to take over their jobs, and many multinationals have this policy,' says **Jim King**. 'Some local staff are too ambitious and think they can take over now, but this is rarely the case. It takes years of building a working relationship and of training and learning before a local staff member can take real responsibility for running a business; very few multinationals have achieved this.' Localization is a valid and important long-term goal for almost all multinationals but, for most, it's so distant on the horizon that it's not even on the timetable. Local staff need to be reminded that it won't happen overnight.

As Kathy Bao of Chung Shing explains, Sunrise's corporate policy is to replace all the Taiwan people based in China with local staff as soon as it can be done. 'One day, we hope we can be 100 per cent local so that we can all go home!,' she jokes. But it's still a very long-term, vague plan.

One exception is Arco China, an oil company originally from the United States that is undertaking extensive exploration and drilling activities. Their joint venture with a Chinese partner is finite: in five years' time, the US partner will basically pull out. It has committed itself to preparing the local staff for this day. 'All our training programs are geared towards localization and replacing ourselves,' explains Arco's Human Resources and Training Director, Tom Pearce. 'As a result, we have a huge and accelerating training schedule, focused on empowerment and raising quality several notches, and constantly reviewing everyone's progress.'

Johnny Ho is also highly committed to localizing, although with far less specific goals. 'All foreign companies in China are trying to localize much of their business, especially in the light of the huge expat costs,' he says. 'There's no particular date we're working towards, but I'm actively trying to promote local staff to higher positions. I'm training them in their jobs, teaching them English. I'm personally not afraid of being replaced by a local person—I would encourage this. Then I can move on, to be GM for the whole of China for my company, for example.' Ho feels that for expats from Hong Kong, Taiwan and elsewhere, 'The next five years, before localization is really widespread, are a window of opportunity for us.

The local people here are so smart, it won't be long before they move up into the jobs now occupied by expats. And their increased pay reflects the rising demand for their services; one of my senior guys was paid RMB 12,000 a month, not a bad salary in China. He just moved on for RMB 18,000.'

Help to realize those expectations
There are several ways to manage staff expectations. You can help local staff to improve their skills in English as a first step, to motivate them to read, write and speak better English before going on to further training. Try to explain PRC staff expectations to your overseas boss and, whenever possible, make a case for some overseas exposure for them (but don't promise what you can't deliver).

Avoid situations where new staff members make assumptions about their entitlements based on what they know about the careers of existing and former staff—many local staff look at the promotions achieved by staff who joined the company before them, and think that they can get promoted just as easily. They don't necessarily realize that companies are not growing so rapidly once they've passed the initial setting-up phase and, in some cases, are not doing so well business-wise.

To inspire your staff, to keep them going, you need to give them a vision to follow—they are looking to you for leadership. You can keep them motivated by a powerful vision, but you shouldn't promise what you can't deliver. You can make the soldiers keep going by the thought of the plum trees, but you'll need to find the plum trees in the end.

During the Three Kingdoms Period, the Emperor of Wei was marching with his troops and, unable to find any water, they became extremely thirsty. He described to them a large and luxuriant grove of plum trees, where the fruit was sour with a tinge of sweetness. The Emperor's description was so detailed and convincing that the soldiers' mouths began to salivate, and they were able to keep advancing.

'Quenching thirst by thinking of plums' (Chinese proverb, Shishuo Xinyu)

PART THREE

Managing in China: Important Working Relationships

Chapter 6

Customers and suppliers

Two of the most important groups of people you will have to deal with in China are customers and suppliers. Make sure your expectations—as well as theirs—are realistic. Education will almost certainly be required, on both sides. You will need to give your staff special training in how to deal with customers and suppliers, and they in their turn will need a little education on how to do business with a Western company.

Customer relations

Dan Shao, in his hair and beauty products import business, has an unusual approach to understanding and educating his customers. 'Chinese respect teachers, so we use the teacher/student relationship to help the customers to understand our products,' Shao explains. 'Our strategy of selling by training is quite popular. The country has been closed for so long, there's so much they don't know; they're trying to connect with the West and they want to understand the Western way of thinking. This is one of the things we explain in training the Chinese salon staff in cosmetics and skin-care products.'

One of Shao's first tasks was to encourage his salon staff to mix with staff from other salons in a training class. 'It was strange for them. They see themselves as territorial—"I have this territory, you have another". They don't want to mix. This is generally the case in China, rather than the competitiveness seen in the USA.'

To a certain extent, the customers will accept this training as advanced learning, and are glad to have the opportunity to learn. However, this is not enough. 'They are mostly encouraged by the chance to make more money,' says Shao. 'Once you tell them they can charge their customers more by providing a better service, they are more interested.'

Shao points out that the American 'fast draw and shoot' way of operating just doesn't work in China. 'If you appear to be in a hurry, you're seen as insincere,' he says. 'You must observe the important rituals, and pay respect to Chinese partners and customers the way they are used to.'

Shao's Shanghainese language skills certainly help him fit in with the locals. 'But, although I understand their language and I'm in many ways close to them, sometimes I don't understand their attitude. For example, the salon professionals don't see themselves as artists, as they do in the West. They see themselves just as workers. I try to emphasize to them that they have unique skills, that the customers come to them individually for their special talents. They take some convincing! I find that you need to compromise less if you speak the local dialect, if you know the local culture. You can get them on your side more, and you can talk to them more like a friend than a foreigner—then you can get them to see the importance of what you are doing.'

For Shao, another important aspect of doing business in China is the need to emphasize the integrity of the product. 'The beauty-care products are expensive, but you can't make them go further by watering them down or diluting them with a cheaper product,' he says. 'To ensure consistent quality and reliability in results, you mustn't tamper with the product. You'd think this was obvious, but to many here, it's not. I have to explain why you must not mess with the products; that once you do it, you damage me and yourself. You can kill the goose which lays the golden eggs.'

One of the ways in which Shao helps customers afford his products is to show them how to increase their productivity. 'I help them to get 48 hours out of 24; how to give really valuable service to the customer. I will sell them a franchise and encourage them and support them, help them to train their assistants, supply everything they need.'

Lay down rules on credit and expenses

Mark Gau, of Sara Lee's China joint venture, feels that, even though customer relations are important, local staff sometimes take it too far. 'For example, we have retail customers—department stores and shops—who haven't paid their bills for some time, even months. But we're still supplying them with goods. We had to implement a much more professional policy about credit limits. Good relationships with these individual customers can be very helpful: they can help to "push" our products and can help us with in-store promotions, etc, but we may reach a point where we have to cut off their credit.' His staff have now begun to recognize the necessity for introducing credit limits; it is important that staff be trained in the area of credit and learn to obey guidelines.

In the same way, you need to set a firm policy on entertainment of customers, before your budget goes through the roof. Although entertaining customers with long, drawn-out banquets and dealing with customers who expect to receive kickbacks are no longer the common occurrences they used to be, they still feature in business life in China. **Alan Chieng** says, 'It used to be the case that you always had to pay under the table to get business in the hotel industry in Beijing. Anyone who wanted to hold a big function would go around all the hotels and give the business to the one which would give them the biggest kickback. To a certain extent, this still happens.'

It is essential that the manager of local staff sets firm policies covering maximum budgets for customer entertainment, the record-keeping requirements for entertainment expenditure and the reporting requirements for all issues concerning the giving and receiving of kickbacks. Ethical issues are a matter for personal judgement and, whatever the manager thinks, it can be difficult to track everything the staff are doing. Bringing issues like kickbacks into the open is an important step in the right direction.

Insist on good service to all

Lee Swee Chee describes his company's approach to maintaining standards of customer service. 'We carry out a customer satisfaction survey every year, and everyone's bonus depends on the level of customer satisfaction achieved. We have cases of customers complaining that our engineers came and didn't do a good job, that we didn't treat the customers very well. Those engineers suffered reduced bonuses. Some service people think they can treat customers badly because the business has already been won. They are not allowed to get away with that here. We have fired staff who don't treat customers right, as a message to the others. On the other hand, we have extra bonuses for those who really satisfy the customers.'

Many customers in China have low expectations because of their country's recent history of lack of choice, lack of product availability, poor quality and poor service. This is now changing, particularly as the China market opens up to Western imported products, overseas competitors arrive to manufacture in China and increasing numbers of Chinese make overseas visits. In all areas of customer service, staff training should emphasize the importance of high standards, not only to keep staff focused but to create new expectations among customers.

Dan Shao feels that China's huge population is partly responsible for the poor attitudes towards personal and individual customer service, and that these attitudes translate into daily life at the hair and beauty salons, his customers. 'The salons in Chinese cities are so big and have so many customers that it's not easy for them to build the kind of customer relationships achieved by salons in the US,' he points out. 'We're trying to teach them that less is more—that you don't necessarily have to get as many customers as possible to be successful and that in fact you can be more profitable by being selective. But you have to see it from their point of view. They have always thought that you should serve the lowest common denominator, and just serve any customer who walks in the door. They have never thought strategically, about which customers are best for them.' Shao is thus teaching about market segmentation and how to add more value to the customer, two concepts still not widely understood in China.

Michael Wu emphasizes the ongoing nature of customer service training, that it never stops. 'I ask all department heads to set an example in constantly improving customer service standards,' he says. 'After the basic training, there's coaching and checking. Many people think that once they've received initial training in customer service, that's enough. But we need to see how they do their jobs, give them constant coaching to improve and maintain improved standards, and let them know that we're watching them, constantly checking their progress. And I check the checkers.'

The Swissotel in Beijing is known for its exemplary customer service and courtesy, and this is achieved through a similar approach of ongoing training and checking. As one guest observed at an extremely upmarket and sophisticated ball held in this hotel, 'The staff are excellent here because they have support; they're not just trained and left [to get on with it]. The expatriate staff are always in the background, not necessarily interfering or taking over the jobs of the local staff—just being there and showing that high standards of customer service are the most important thing.'

In his campaign for improved customer service, **Mark Thomas** not only wrote a manual on the ideal quality standards for running a health club but he adapted the concepts into tasks to be performed by all staff. 'We had a big pile of training manuals and quality standards manuals; I wanted to simplify these and make it easier for the staff. So I defined three areas of quality standards—service, friendliness and cleanliness—which encompass everything in the club. I identified service as the weakest area; assessing the existing levels of standards has allowed me to concentrate on improving this area. My approach is to use hands-on management—whenever I see service breaking down, I try to resolve the situation and then use it as a training test case. However, this means that when I'm not around, things don't run so smoothly, so I have to work on improving my supervisors.'

In many businesses across China, local staff working in the area of customer service have shown a tendency to be polite to foreigners but a reluctance to extend the same politeness to other local PRC Chinese. This was particularly apparent in the hotel industry when foreign-managed hotels first opened their doors in China, notably in Beijing. Alan Chieng of Swissotel says, 'Local staff generally don't like to serve local people, and to a certain extent this will never change. They always assume that foreigners are the boss in any mixed group. We have a Western lady in our office to deal with the Western customers, and any locals coming into our office always assume automatically that she's the boss. We never tolerate rudeness to guests under any circumstances, but staff are never rude to foreigners. Any instances of rudeness to guests—which results in instant dismissal—has only ever been to local guests. They are also the most sensitive to it.'

Your PRC staff need to be trained and constantly reminded that *all* customers have to be treated with courtesy. Mark Thomas is keen to establish good relations between members and staff and insists that his staff treat Western and Chinese members and guests equally well. So far, he has experienced few difficulties. He also wants his club to be seen as impartial. 'By contrast, there's a pub in Shanghai which has pub games. They charge a deposit if you want to borrow the game to play, but only if you're a local, not if you're a foreigner. I can see why they do this, but it's not fair, and I wouldn't want to have such practices in my club.'

Establish a discounts policy
Setting a discounts policy for customers is not difficult; however, implementing it is. Customers in China have a tendency to ask for discounts beyond those stated in your policy, however generous you are. You must see this from their point of view—it's all part of their need for 'face'. If you make them feel special, such as by giving them a discount '...which we only give to special customers', this

gives them what they want. Also, in many cases, they'll be expected to report to their boss that they were successful in 'getting a good price'.

Be seen to stick to the rules, but try to find ways of making customers feel special that don't involve giving discounts but do give them a story to tell their boss. Enlist the help of your staff here, especially if you're a Westerner; they'll probably know far more about pleasing local customers than you do.

Avoid abuse of customer privileges

Kathy Bao says, 'Customers behave very differently in China than they do in Taiwan, in my experience. For instance, customers know we have a policy of accepting goods and making refunds if goods are not satisfactory. But in China, the customers would return a pair of shoes to the shop having bought them three months ago and worn them every day since, and complain that they are broken and make a scene in the shop. In Taiwan, we would accept returned goods after one week only, and the customers understand this.' Bao has also noticed the tendency of PRC customers to try and bargain, when all the prices at Sunrise are fixed.

Lee Swee Chee says, 'In many ways, China is not credit-worthy. We always make sure we get paid before we ship any goods. The law in China will not protect you, you must protect yourself. It's only too easy to have a collection problem and a heap of bad debts in China.'

The safest way to do business is by strict payment terms of cash in advance. Especially in providing a service, companies who charge all or part of the payment in advance are giving themselves a double advantage: more cash flow upfront as well as avoiding possible non-payment. However, in a service situation—much more than in the purchase of more tangible, manufactured items—some local customers want to decide if it's what they want before paying, and some just want to enjoy the benefits without parting with their cash. Avoid giving your customers the chance to rip you off by insisting on upfront payment. You must occasionally be tough and turn away customers, but they'll soon get the message and abide by your rules. By making the Chinese consumer aware of how a Western supplier operates, you'll be doing other companies a favour.

Know your customers
Kathy Bao finds that shopping in China, much more so than in Taiwan, is a relaxing recreational activity, a family outing; people come to her store, Sunrise, to eat out as well as shop. So Bao has provided a large food court in the store. 'Fast food and eating-out generally are seen as more special in China than in Taiwan, and they still have novelty value. Our prices, at RMB 12 for a bowl of noodles, may seem cheap, but it must be remembered that many people here would usually pay only RMB 2. We need to bear this in mind when providing services to customers in China. The market is certainly not as mature as Hong Kong or Taiwan, even in the big cities like Shanghai and Beijing.'

If you're selling a new product or service, you must take care in explaining the features and benefits of what you are providing, because if the customers don't understand what it is they are getting and the purpose behind it, they simply won't like it. If you're providing a Western-style training class, for example, and the customers expect a Chinese-style one, they'll be disappointed and unhappy. You need to explain upfront what you are providing—don't assume Chinese consumers read the promotional or sales materials. Because customers in China still have a fairly limited exposure to the more sophisticated products and services, they tend to think in the old way, and it's your job to educate them.

Michael Wu warns against making certain assumptions about customers in China. 'You must remember that, in China, what the customers want may not be the same as in Hong Kong or Singapore, and may be totally different to the US or Canada. As we want all our customers to be happy, we must be sensitive to their particular needs. For example, when we serve a Chinese banquet, I have trained the staff to leave time between courses and to clear away each course before serving the next. But in one particular case, the customers, local businessmen from Guangzhou, complained. They didn't like the food to be served this way; they wanted all the courses to be served in rapid succession, with piles of food all over the table. They wanted to impress their guests that they were treating them to all this food, so much that they couldn't finish it. But Western customers, including many Hong Kong and Singapore people, wouldn't like this.' So Wu finds it necessary to train his staff not just in what he regards as traditional standards of service at a good hotel, but in the varying needs of different customers.

Michael Sengol, another Holiday Inn general manager who has worked in Shanghai, shares another story of customer service in China. 'We had a guest who ordered shark's fin soup, so we brought him a bowl. He was most unhappy, and initially we couldn't work out why. "But, sir," we said, "this is our best shark's fin—we have cooked it according to the traditional recipe, and usually our guests are delighted!" But the customer continued to be dissatisfied. It finally transpired that his problem was that the shark's fin soup, the most expensive dish on the menu, was brought in a plain bowl without ceremony. He needed more "face", more attention to the fact that he was a wealthy and prosperous customer. He wanted the shark's fin to be brought in a big silver bowl, on a big silver tray, with several waiters in attendance. The soup itself was not important—what was important was that he had the money to order the most expensive dish on the menu.'

Working with suppliers

Unlike the situation in many Western countries, out-sourcing your supplies may not be the best answer in China. Expatriate managers need to understand the advantages of in-sourcing as an alternative.

Michael Wu, when he first started working at the Holiday Inn in Guangzhou, found that in-sourcing was more reliable than out-sourcing. 'In many countries, you can bring in external help from outside suppliers for aspects of maintenance, engineering, special catering, housekeeping and for special guests services, such as a beauty salon. But in China, such services of the quality I need often aren't available. We have to provide everything ourselves, to be entirely self-sufficient.'

Four years later, Wu finds the situation is slowly improving and limited out-sourcing is becoming possible due to the fact that better-quality products and services are available. Suppliers, once found, must be carefully managed, however. 'We do a market survey of food items every 10 days, based on quotations received from our suppliers, and we go to the markets and check the prices. This is a tedious job and may be a waste of time. In theory, we get the best quality at the best prices, but in reality our purchasers probably still just go to their favourite supplier. However, I interview regular contractors myself, to try to satisfy myself that they are reliable and honest.'

The move from in-sourcing to out-sourcing at Holiday Inn is slow and experimental, however. 'It's a balancing act; we're not sure if it will work. For example, we're contracting out the job of relocating our business centre to the executive floor; we'll see how it goes before we try anything else.'

Choose your suppliers carefully

Quelle, a well-known German company that produces a mail order catalogue, has extensive sourcing operations all over China. The opening-up of the economy of China over the last 10 years has led to a much wider choice of suppliers. Quelle's Simon Aliband says, 'With the arrival of the market economy, if suppliers don't perform, we can get rid of them and try someone else, which is a big change for anyone doing business in China. There is so much more choice.'

Remember that suppliers in China are in a weaker position now. 'It used to be that China could win big contracts for supplying many items because Chinese prices were rock-bottom,' continues Aliband. 'Quality was not great but, to a certain extent, the cheap prices made up for this. However, now that raw material prices have gone up and quality standards are increasing around Asia, China is having to compete with every other country in the region. Meanwhile, it is held back by its moribund socialist system, so it can't liberalize foreign trade completely, and huge numbers of people are working fairly unproductively in huge State-owned factories linked to the import–export corporations, which reduces China's competitive edge. This is now changing, but slowly.'

Many China-based suppliers still just expect orders to roll in without any effort on their part, especially in innovation, and also expect the import–export corporations to handle their marketing. Aliband advises that if you want good quality supplies, you must go directly to the factory where they are made, and educate the workers directly in what you want and expect. You can't leave it to your supplier to do this for you—you must be much more hands-on.

Aliband emphasizes the importance of building strong relationships with suppliers to ensure quality and reliability, working on the level of a partnership on a long-term basis, and showing them the potential amount of business that could be directed their way if it all works out. But warn them very clearly about the high standards they must meet. 'You should test them with a small order first,' Aliband says, 'and not just do a factory evaluation, but look at their management. Also, make sure they own their own factory and that this is where the goods will be made, not contracted out to someone else.'

The sign of a good factory is *not* one where workers say, 'Yes, yes, we can do it!', but where they say they can do it (and they will always say this) but with some hesitation and reservations, which you can then examine in detail. 'Look for a motivated work-force and a clean working area,' recommends Aliband, 'otherwise you'll have plenty of rejects on quality and cleanliness. Look for clear quality control processes, not just the presence of quality control people—every factory has QC people, and many have no idea what they're doing. With the increasing popularity of ISO 9000 [the international quality standard certification system], people have much more of an idea about what quality means, although many are still not doing much about it. Show the factory people the actual products that you consider acceptable, so they'll have a very clear idea of exactly what you expect and require.'

When choosing a supplier, it's common to ask a factory to show you samples of its work; in many cases, these will be poor, even worse than the usual offerings. The factory will have many excuses for this, such as, 'We sold all the best ones', 'This is the end of the production run', and 'This is an off-cut'. Take this as a warning, Aliband says. 'You don't want to wait a long time till they get it right, nor can you afford a high reject rate. The success of your business may depend on these suppliers and they must be reliable from the outset.'

Chinese factories have a tendency to make their contracts as vague and woolly as possible, so you must pin them down to exact definitions of quality. Aliband notes that the usual roles of buyers and sellers in Europe are reversed in China. 'What the seller would do in Europe, the buyer does in China—such as quality checking and making sure the amount delivered is the same as the amount invoiced. Sellers in China are arrogant— they expect you to fit in with their requirements. This didn't matter a few years ago, when there was no competition and their prices were the lowest. But they are finding that they can't behave like this any more. They will now have to start monitoring quality themselves, not just expect us to do it.'

Be specific with your orders

Lee Swee Chee says, 'In dealing with local suppliers in China, it's important to hold back a portion of the final payment until you make sure you are satisfied with the work, which I guess is really the same as anywhere else. For example, we had a problem with our telephone system but, because we'd already paid for everything, the suppliers were not in the least interested in helping us. By contrast, with our office decoration suppliers, we held back the last 10 per cent to make sure they would come back and sort out any last-minute problems; this worked out well.'

It is a good idea for all companies dealing with local suppliers to be specific when spelling out quality and maintenance requirements, and to educate them in what they can and cannot expect from you. Withholding part of the payment is a rather unsophisticated way of ensuring requirements are met, but it does seem to work.

Set a policy on supplier selection
Kathy Bao explains that Sunrise sells Chung Shing's own products and other merchandise, all manufactured in China. 'Most of this, 80 per cent, is brought in from other companies. There is now an increased number of suppliers in Shanghai, and the quality is improving. The prices are much lower than in Taiwan.'

The store has a policy on the selection of suppliers, which includes reviewing their products and performance regularly. Around 40 per cent of the store's suppliers are the same ones who supplied the store when it opened in 1992. However, Bao says, 'Twice a year, we reselect suppliers, based on their pricing, quality, product range, and if the clothes, for example, are suitable for summer or winter. If the suppliers are no good, we drop them. We explain to them the reasons for this, and it should help them to improve. It is essential to be quite tough with suppliers in China.'

Train your staff in how to deal with suppliers
When sending staff out to make purchases, Lee Swee Chee insists on three quotations for each item over a certain amount; the accounts department will check up on invoices. He always challenges staff if he thinks the payments are too large for the item concerned. Cash transactions are minimized by using a bank transfer system, and all managers have limits on the payments they can approve. There is an internal audit every year, and any major problems are reported to the head of Honeywell Asia-Pacific.

Lee feels that the best safeguard against fraud is to show people that they can have a very good career with the company if they work well and show honesty and integrity. Any lack of honesty results in instant dismissal. Secondly, Lee points to the importance of having high-quality and reliable finance staff.

Thu Ho finds that when staff are involved in purchasing, 'It's very hard to avoid them developing relationships with certain suppliers and then pushing those products to continue receiving incentives and building their *guanxi*. The only solution is to encourage competitive quotes to get the most reasonable price, and to change suppliers frequently. Meanwhile, we have a fund for staff to entertain suppliers, which everyone shares openly.'

Mark Gau has a novel approach to dealing with the age-old problem of what to do when suppliers offer kickbacks or inducements to his staff. 'We have a policy which actually was used by the old enterprise, before Sara Lee took over, which says that everyone must tell the GM about any kickback they've been offered. Then the GM decides if you can keep it, or if it should go into a separate fund which everyone shares.'

The company also has a strict policy that three bids must be received before any supplier is chosen for a large project. Also, suppliers are regularly changed and the purchasing department is kept quite separate from quality control. 'If you have a clean purchasing department and an independent quality inspection department, even independent from the GM, then you much reduce the offering of kickbacks from suppliers. And you should always keep the accounting person separate from the person who authorizes payments. You must have checks to make sure that nothing deviates from the standard procedure. This is a policy we have adopted from our US operation—it actually protects people and enables the company to trust them to do jobs on their own.

'We have to accept that multinational reporting and planning systems are here to stay, and we have to demonstrate to our staff that the process helps us to manage the business better. We also have to show that the close control and monitoring systems that are used in multinationals are actually for the good of the staff, as well as for the good of the company.'

Insist on the highest standards

Thu Ho explains that most of RAAS's raw materials still have to be imported. With those items that are sourced locally, Ho finds it necessary to send quality assurance staff to the suppliers' factories to watch them. She says, 'You must reject those items which are even the slightest bit substandard. Get them to produce more basic items, like packaging materials, and import the more problematic items, like filters and chemicals. And if the suppliers insist that the next production run will be better, you shouldn't necessarily believe them. It may be just as bad.'

If Chinese suppliers are constantly reminded that you will reject anything that is not of the highest quality, they are more likely to pay attention to improving their standards. Let them know that you are aware of their tendency to deliver goods or services that are substandard (and of their expectation that they will get away with it) and rigorously inspect every item in every consignment.

Chapter 7

Your Chinese partner and your boss

Two of the most important working relationships you will have as a manager in China are those with your Chinese partner and your boss. Both have the potential to make or break you, so you need to be very careful, at least in the initial stages of your career in China. If you demonstrate sensitivity and understanding, and don't push too hard, you will gain the trust and respect of your Chinese partner, and from there continue to enjoy a good working relationship. The situation with your boss is somewhat different—you want sensitivity and understanding to be shown to you! However, there are ways in which you can lower unrealistic expectations and still maintain a good relationship.

Your Chinese partner

Kathy Bao's staff in the Sunrise Department Store still maintain their relationship with the staff at the 'mother store', and tend to go to them with their problems. 'I wish they would come to us more,' says Bao, 'but gradually they are beginning to trust us.' The 'mother store', or Chinese partner, owns 30 per cent of Sunrise, and is no longer active in the running of the Sunrise Store. But, as Bao says, 'They helped us a lot at the beginning to change the mentality of the staff, and it would have been more difficult without them.'

Bao strongly emphasizes the importance of establishing and maintaining a good relationship with one's joint venture partner, and seeking the advice and recommendations of the local municipal government in finding one in the first place. Certainly, if you are in a joint venture situation, it pays to work with your Chinese partner and use them to help, rather than hinder, your business.

Build a positive relationship

Michael Wu's hotel in Guangzhou is jointly owned by Singaporean and PRC interests, and managed by Holiday Inn. All three parties had to agree to his appointment as general manager. 'Some overseas Chinese and other foreigners in China think it's unpleasant to have to work with and talk to a Chinese partner. Actually, we've now found that it's quite a positive experience. We call them "Party A". This used to be a bit of a joke, but I've discovered that once I established a relationship with them, I have gained them as an ally and they are very useful to me. They give me a lot of good advice.'

Wu warns against trying to build relationships with your PRC partner through giving them expensive meals or gifts. 'This may have worked 10 years ago, but it doesn't work any more, especially in the big cities. They know whether it's sincere or not, and it can create the wrong impression. It's better to be sincere and open with them, to seek their advice, and build a relationship with them through honestly sharing problems.'

Wu finds that his relationship with his Chinese partners is improving, mainly because, 'They're becoming more capitalistic, more open-minded, more modern in their thinking. We are now more on the same wavelength. For example, I recently went on holiday to the US and brought back four neckties—one for the chairman of the Chinese partner, two for the Chinese partner's deputy general managers and one for myself. I thought I would let them choose which tie they liked, and I would keep the one that no-one wanted. Actually, they chose the ones I liked least. Four years ago, I don't think they would have liked any of them! Their taste is definitely improving, from my point of view, and this means we're closer. This may seem like a small, inconsequential story, but it seemed quite significant to me at the time.'

One Shanghai-based Hong Kong Chinese property manager who runs a property and consulting business has made her Chinese partner a real member of the team. 'Some people prefer their Chinese partner to be very passive, to not get involved, to just make them legal and leave them to it. But this is not making use of your partner. Mine is very useful for his local *guanxi* and his ability to help me manage local staff. He sits in the office and takes care of

177

things while I'm away. He's warm and friendly and all my customers know and like him, and respect him for his role. He enjoys cooking and even comes to my home to cook dinner, special Shanghai dishes such as Shanghai Hairy Crabs, for myself and my guests. He's such an asset in so many ways.'

Understand the cultural differences
Some of the most difficult aspects of joint venture partner management relate to cultural differences. One US company taking over a local business in Shanghai found that many Chinese businesses are run in a very family-oriented way with the boss behaving like an emperor. An executive of this company says, 'Our general manager, once the entrepreneur–owner of the factory, still feels that it's his personal fiefdom. To a certain extent, we must let him carry on. We don't want him to feel that his status is diminished, but we must also now run the business as part of a multinational. We try to treat him as a very close friend, and show him that his job is secure and that we want him to be successful.'

However, implementing change takes time. As this executive adds, 'In China, people think of only incremental change and cannot imagine dramatic change. For example, if you are riding a horse but you need to go faster, you just beat the horse until he runs faster. You wouldn't think of changing to a car!'

Keep your Chinese partner informed
Michael Wu finds that it's important to keep your 'Party A' informed, even on minor matters. If in doubt, tell them about it anyway. When Wu asked his deputy engineer to

stay in the hotel when the chief engineer was away, and allowed him to have free meals with his wife in the hotel, he thought this would be OK, and didn't bother to consult with Party A. But Party A didn't agree. Afterwards, Wu realized the importance of keeping the PRC partner involved in the decision-making process, particularly in anything to do with the staff.

'When I was dragged into Party A's office, and shown quite clearly their displeasure, this was a big lesson for me. I decided not to fight, but to listen to their sensitivities. It became clear that they want to support the interests of the local staff, and they want to see fair treatment. They don't want to set precedents which may be open to abuse. I never thought of this, but when I explained why I did it, they respected my motives. Now, I ask them before I do anything. It now helps me a lot to have them on my side. They now also tell me a lot about what's going on, more than I would know without them.'

Understand their objectives

Not all Chinese partners want to make money. They don't want to make losses but, in the China context, there are many reasons why Chinese parties become owners of enterprises, and they don't always include profit.

For example, the Swissotel in Beijing is owned substantially by the Hong Kong and Macau Affairs Office, bankrolled by the Bank of China. The Office asked Swissotel to run the hotel under a management contract. All the Office's big functions, such as meetings of the Advisory Board established to assist with the future administration of Hong Kong, are held in the hotel. The Office is concerned about the room rates being charged, but not much else—it sees the hotel only as a place in which to hold its functions. As a result, the hotel is less profit-oriented than a foreign-owned hotel. Because there's not such a drive to be cost-conscious, the hotel employs 32 expatriates, many of whom are Europeans, as compared with the China World Hotel which has 42 expatriate staff but is three times the size.

Many Chinese partners are obsessed with control and knowing about what's going on. This means that in many organizations there are a number of 'spies' in prominent positions acting for the Chinese partner. At one Beijing hotel, an expatriate hotel department manager says, 'There are at least nine, all in senior jobs, who mostly sit around drinking coffee. I don't think it looks very good for the discipline of the staff, especially in front of guests. They just talk to the local staff, they don't talk to the expats, and they only come in useful when we have an inspection from the fire department, the hygiene department and the Public Security Bureau.'

These 'spies' are just keeping an eye on the organization for the benefit of the Chinese partner, the owner, and ultimately the Communist Party. They are a way of life for all joint ventures and PRC-owned, but foreign-managed, businesses. They fulfil the objective of many Chinese partners, which is to closely monitor what's going on and to have control.

Remember, what's in it for them?
A manufacturer based in Shanghai says, 'The best way to deal with your Chinese partner is to be flexible, go along

with them, give them face, let them take the lead, help them to get what they want—as long as your profit is not adversely affected. In our case, they get a bonus based on our profits, although the Government still gets a bigger share. Now that State-owned operations in China are encouraged to make money, this is more important to them. So our Chinese partners are becoming more commercially minded—we actively help them here by explaining what's happening and helping them to understand.'

Chinese partners are looking for status as well as money in their dealings with Western organizations. Make sure you invite them to all the important functions, ask them to make speeches and introduce them to all key foreign visitors.

Your boss

Craig Pepples often finds himself struggling with unrealistic expectations from his head office. Fuelled by media hype, expectations in the Western world are that anyone can succeed in business in China and that profits will rocket. Pepples has a boss who believes he can perform miracles, that he '...should double the profits and grow the business by more than 100 per cent each year because the newspapers and magazines are full of China and how it's booming'. Pepples says, 'I've increased our business by 65 per cent over last year but there's such media hype that my boss is almost disappointed. You should remember that you are in a better position than they are to know the actual situation of your business in China. True figures here are almost impossible to come by. No-one knows more than anyone else does.'

Keep your boss informed of your situation honestly and accurately to combat this misconception. The tough thing is you may not even know what the boss is reading, because few business magazines and books are easily available in China. One solution is to ask friends in Hong Kong, Europe, the States and elsewhere to send you clippings, so at least you can anticipate the next round of even more ambitious media-fed demands that emanate from head office!

Educate, explain and inform

It's no good pathetically exclaiming, 'But you don't understand China!' This won't get you anywhere. It will just serve to make your boss feel more and more insecure and anxious about this expensive, volatile, unpredictable subsidiary or other operation he or she has in the world's largest market. You've got to help your boss understand the differences between operating in China and operating at head office, and the need to blend cultures. Start from scratch, make no assumptions and, like any other kind of training, keep up the process of reinforcement and review.

One problem is that many head office operations don't have a spokesman for China or, even worse, they may have somebody they think is a spokesman but who actually is not. For example, one American company in China used to ask their China country manager to attend their board meetings and give them a picture of the China scene. He became too busy running the China operation to keep flying down to the board meetings so, when the company promoted a Hong Kong Chinese to the board, they asked this person to do the job instead. But, like many

Hong Kong people, this executive was quite uncomfortable with, and ignorant of, operations on the mainland. However, his Chinese face and the fact that his parents were born in Guangdong Province meant that he was always looked to for comments whenever China was mentioned. So, the mystique and misunderstandings continue.

Jim King found he needed to explain to his boss that there are enormous cultural differences which affect the way one can operate in China. Also, he says, there are government differences, infrastructure differences and mindset differences. All of these have huge implications for the establishment of a corporate culture and a profitable business in China.

As William Hanbury-Tenison of Jardine Matheson explains, you can't set up exactly the same operation in China as you might do in Hong Kong or the UK, or anywhere else, for that matter, however much the bosses at headquarters may pressure you. For foreign companies, it must be a blend of their existing corporate culture and the requirements of the China business scene, and the needs and expectations of the local staff. This must be explained to bosses from the outset.

Irene Wolinski of General Motors in Beijing concurs. 'The problem is,' she says, 'that the executives from the US come to China, import the whole operation and try to just drop it into the China context, hoping it will work as well as it does in the United States. Because it *does* work in the States, they're afraid to change anything in case that doesn't work. They kind of know that they should make some adjustments to the China context, but they don't know how to modify their existing operation. And all their consultants are from the US, so they're not helpful. In fact, the consultants are trying to learn about China from their clients! There's a real need to understand the China context and achieve a mix of both; everyone knows this, but the big challenge is how to achieve it without losing the things that work.'

Jim King says that when you have a successful joint venture in China, it's because the foreign partner accommodated the local Chinese partner, and didn't force them to operate in a manner similar to the one with which they were familiar back at home. He quotes an example. 'The Hewlett Packard joint venture has been in existence for over 10 years now, and is widely seen as one of the most well-established, effective and successful in China, frequently quoted as an excellent case. But much of this success is the result of accommodation and adaptation to the China scene, rather than rigidly adhering to the US model.'

Kathy Bao finds China altogether less predictable than working in her native Taiwan, and has to keep explaining the implications of this to the parent company. 'The results here are never what you expect,' she says, 'mainly because people here have no idea of the kind of quality standards and taste we expect, although this is changing. When you ask for something, you must show them very clearly what you have in mind.' For example, Bao wanted flowers to decorate the store at the grand opening event which the bosses from Taiwan were attending. The staff bought garishly coloured plastic blooms, thinking these were nice enough. Bao was appalled. 'But it was not their fault; they weren't to know that I didn't want them.'

Another time, Bao asked factory staff if they could produce a series of ladies' clothes for the office, originally designed in Europe. They said they could, but the results were disappointing. 'Unlike Taiwan, there is a tendency in China to insist that anything can be done, without a realistic understanding of what is really possible or not possible,' says Bao, who has to explain all this back home.

Like senior management anywhere, CEOs and other big bosses hate being taken by surprise, especially if it's bad news—they don't even like good news sometimes, unless they know it's coming. Keep in touch with head office, delivering both good and bad news, if only to give them some comfort that they know what's going on.

One of the toughest situations in which expats can find themselves is when they take a job at an existing joint venture or wholly-owned China operation and find they have inherited a problem where the foreign investors have put in too much money and are expecting big returns quickly. It just isn't possible. Dominic Tang found himself in such a situation, and found that it was definitely 'lose-lose'. 'They offered me a huge salary, expensive housing and a car, and expected miracles. They just hadn't done their homework on what was possible in China. When the executives they put in failed to deliver what they expected, they fired them—if they hadn't resigned already. I followed a string of such executives. It was hopeless.'

The reverse scenario, one where there has been too little investment, can also make your job as a manager in China highly problematic. How to reach profit targets if you can't hire enough staff, haven't got space to accommodate the ones you can hire, haven't got enough computers or telephone lines for them, and you and 85 other staff members have to share two fax machines? How will your staff feel if the office environment is so poor it seems as if they're back working for a State-owned company, although this foreign company expects them to work much harder?

Neither scenario is uncommon in China, and neither is satisfactory for the expats concerned or for their bosses back at headquarters. 'An inadequate investment, a meanness in setting up in China and a feeling that the only good thing about China is its cheap labour, are fairly common attitudes among Hong Kong and Taiwan companies in China,' says Tang. 'That's why it's quite difficult for them to hire staff. They have this reputation for low pay and bad working conditions.'

Spell out your targets and time-frame
Lee Swee Chee advises, 'Don't commit to achieving 100 per cent growth every year and give yourself impossible targets. The headquarters office will then give you a hard time if you don't make it. And don't get burned by promising to make money fast. Start small and grow with the market. Don't grow too much before you're ready, but don't be so conservative that the demands on your business are greater than your infrastructure and you can't meet the business obligations you've got. We have month-by-month business analyses to see where we're going, and we

keep our fingers on the pulse of the market. We neither want to expand too quickly nor not quickly enough; it's not easy to forecast what will happen in this market.'

Dominic Tang feels that one of the biggest problems confronting foreign companies in China is that senior management at head office in, for example, the United States or Europe, '...have no idea about China. They did no homework, have over-invested, and now they expect you to make them a fast return. They then suffer a big turnover in their management team, because they just can't achieve the results the bosses want. The objectives they set are impossible, but they won't listen to their people on the ground.'

In Tang's experience, US-based companies are the worst offenders when it comes to impossible demands. 'They are less liable to be strategically minded when it comes to China,' he says. 'They insist on short-term results, and are obsessed with quarterly profits.' On joining a European company, he found the time-frames more realistic. 'But it's your job to educate your boss!'

Stress the constraints—and the potential
Craig Pepples talks about the 'two billion armpits' syndrome that affects senior management at head office and makes them persist in having unrealistic profit expectations. 'In the late 1980s and early 1990s, head offices of multinationals were really going crazy about profit expectations from China. There was the story of the deodorant salesman looking at the China market, and all he could think was, "Wow! Two billion armpits!", without thinking that not everyone will buy deodorant. Meanwhile, his boss

is saying, "Why aren't you selling 1.5 billion tubes of deodorant?" Now, there will be the "Chuppies", the Chinese yuppies, who will buy luxury items like this, but they are the tip of the iceberg, they are only a very small percentage of the whole.'

Pepples feels that it is essential to remind outsiders that, in reality, the buying power of the China consumer is still very low—bosses, in particular, need to be reminded of this. In China, the per capita income is lower than that of Indonesia. 'Sometimes, it suits the Chinese authorities to "cook the books" and make out that people in China are very prosperous; at other times, they would rather show a more accurate picture, of poverty and backwardness, and of sixteenth-century living conditions. In any case, Chinese statistics are confusing: one set of statistics is issued by the Customs Authorities and is usually at odds with the set published by MOFERT, the Ministry of Foreign Economic Relations and Trade. No attempt is made by the authorities to resolve discrepancies. It is small wonder that those working in China, as well as their bosses at home, are confused about profit expectations.'

On customer relations, Jim King comments that, although customers in his industry (high technology) are globally becoming more alike, the way he communicates with and approaches customers in China is still very different. 'For example, in a 30-minute meeting with customers in the US, I can identify their needs, priorities and objections, and make an initial sales presentation. But here in China, it can take many visits to the customer to even get to the first stage of finding out their needs, and then, a number of banquets and social occasions to get the same results as you would in 30 minutes in the US.'

So if your boss expects you to make six sales calls a day, and to make at least one sale out of every five calls, you'll have to explain it's impossible. It just takes more time, and more *guanxi*-building, than is required in most other countries. However, despite all these difficulties, it is worth keeping your boss mindful of the great potential of the China market.

'China has the biggest growth prospects for our company right now,' says Craig Pepples. 'This is true for many other businesses today.' India is arguably not yet ready, and Malaysia and Indonesia don't have the size of population or such extensive development prospects. 'There is no other market now with such fantastic upward potential as China.' Don't forget that yourself, and don't let your boss forget it, either.

Support your local staff
On the subject of staff management, **Patrick Un** considers that the biggest challenge is to bridge the gap between what the boss expects and what the local people can deliver. 'You must match expectations. Most managers in joint ventures and representative offices are still foreigners. What is the nature of the gap between their expectations and those of their staff? Once you have answered this question, you must introduce steps or stages towards closing the gap. And this means a lot of guidance and support. For example, we had a visit from a vice president from head office. The staff made a good job of organizing the meeting, but no-one thought of picking him up at the

airport. They just don't realize it's their job to think of all the details. They don't do any jobs except those you specifically ask them to do.'

Craig Pepples also has to face high expectations from his head office about what staff can and cannot deliver. 'Head office think about their staff in Hong Kong and their expatriates, and expect the local PRC staff to be like them. To head office, it looks like the China staff are doing a pathetic job. But they're actually doing a very good job, in the circumstances. They are paid much less and, frankly, they're less efficient and less productive. It's our job as expatriates to stop them from feeling like failures and to help them to be more productive and more efficient. I have to mediate between head office expectations about staff and the staff themselves, trying not to demotivate the staff and trying to help head office to see the true picture.'

Welcome visits from head office

Some expats live in dread of a visit from headquarters. However, this can be a blessing in disguise, especially if you can use the occasion to argue for improved conditions and more investment, and to *educate* your boss about your situation. Neither complain constantly nor play down your problems, but show factual evidence to support your arguments.

Introduce your boss to your staff, and impress upon your staff the importance of the visit; get them to wear their best clothes and rehearse with them the kind of answers they should give to questions. Don't tell them exactly what to say, but try to avoid negativity and encourage them to show enthusiasm and commitment. Make your boss feel that you, *their* boss, are making good progress in bringing on local staff and leading a team of bright young locals who have been clearly well-selected and well-trained.

Craig Pepples encourages visits from his CEO and chairman so that they can find out for themselves the real situation in China. 'They come here and look and listen; they can see my way of thinking, and they can follow my line of reasoning afterwards, when they have left. We used to work on my twice-yearly objectives for China sitting in the chairman's garden near the Peak in Hong Kong; it was so out of place. Now they come to me in Shanghai for these meetings. This is much more appropriate: it really gets them to see my situation—the reality is right here.

'After we moved my objective-setting meetings to China, we began to achieve major breakthroughs. My CEO was on the outside, not me, and it's usually the person on the outside who's able to see the wood for the trees, who has the insights. This is a good position for your boss to be in. We then had really useful discussions. She could see we had all these salespeople, around 90, but their productivity, their volume of business, was around the same as for 16 salespeople in the US. Yet I was in this trap of hiring more and more salespeople. She said to me, "Stop hiring and try improving their productivity!" Mostly, when your performance is reviewed by your boss, you go into *their* inner sanctum. It's so much better if they come to yours, although not every CEO will make the effort or feel it's appropriate.'

Don't play down your circumstances
As we have seen, China is no longer a hardship posting. However, you are still making sacrifices in relocating to the Middle Kingdom, especially if you moved from a more comfortable place. Neither exaggerate nor minimize the personal inconveniences, but put your boss clearly in the picture when you describe what it is like living and working in China. The infrastructure problems, the limitations surrounding shopping and entertainment, inexperienced staff and the difficulties in getting around, all take their toll on expats, and everyone should allow themselves six to nine months to settle in.

Having said that, you are ready for the challenge and you want to do a good job in China. Make sure you get what you deserve, you earn every cent of your salary—a fact your head office should be reminded of, frequently.

PART FOUR

Managing in China: Your Personal Life

Chapter 8

Family, friends and entertainment

Surviving in China is all about not being isolated and not restricting yourself to the expat world. Don't assume that the things you used to do at home just can't be done here. After some time and effort, and without breaking the law, most things are possible. You can watch English-language movies; you can have your pet dogs and cats with you; you can have all your books and furniture from home with you. Don't give yourself needless hardships. However, do assume that you'll be in China for a while and make yourself as settled and comfortable as possible. Although much around you will seem rather bizarre (as mentioned earlier), you can create your own familiar world. The most common excuse for not doing this is lack of time, so make time to establish a base for yourself before you get into full-time work.

Somewhere to live

Kathy Bao of Chung Shing didn't initially intend to stay long in China; she found the going tough when she first started visiting Shanghai. 'I stayed in a hotel for the first six months. I had no friends, and there was nothing to do after work—I just tended to meet other Taiwanese expats,' she recalls. 'But since then, there is much more to do and I know more people in Shanghai, but you must make an effort.' At first, Bao thought she would just set up the store and then leave, but 'I didn't realize I would stay, and now I realize I can't leave!'

Leave that hotel
It's easy for those who stay in a hotel for any length of time to get settled and just stay there. If you camp out in a hotel and wait 'for a while' before finding an apartment, you can easily begin to feel ambivalent about staying in China, and that feeling of ambivalence transmits itself to your local staff. **Thu Ho** lived in the Sheraton Hua Ting in Shanghai for six years before taking the plunge and moving to an apartment, where she now feels much more settled.

Two Italian expatriates working with an oil company deliberately lived in a hotel all their time in China, because they found the local scene 'too difficult'. With a complete lack of Chinese language skills, no knowledge or interest in China or things Chinese (they spent much of their time in the only Italian restaurant in the city), they faced what they described as appalling problems trying to negotiate with their potential joint venture partner. But they were, all along, sending out the wrong signals—that they were not staying, they were just passing through.

When you rent an apartment in China, you learn a lot about the country and how it works (or, in some cases, doesn't work). You learn about shopping, deliveries, paying bills, hiring an *ayi*, travelling to work, the electrics, the plumbing—just about everything there is to know about domestic life in China. You may think that these are things you'd prefer not to know about, but it really is a help in your future job of 'managing in China'.

Live close to work

Walking or cycling to work provides the advantages of exercise and understanding a little bit more about the locality in which your office is situated, and can ensure that you're reasonably likely to get to work on time. Of course, having a car and driver is a huge perk, but again it does put a big strain on the budget and the pressure for profitability. And it can get stuck in the traffic, anywhere. The best thing about this arrangement is that the driver can take care of parking, and you can avoid having to hunt for taxis. A good driver can also double-up as a Mr Fix-It and a shopping and restaurant expert, which can be great for looking after visitors. But watch those costs!

Weigh up the costs of accommodation

Jim King feels it is best to be prepared to lower your expectations about your living standards, and not mind that your apartment is not so large or well-appointed as it might have been in the United States or elsewhere.

Some expats make the most of their housing allowances and spend huge sums on extravagant properties. Over US$7000 per month is not unusual in Beijing for a court-yard house: it's very beautiful and has plenty of room, but is the cost really justified for a single person, and one who is constantly on business trips? If the company is paying, many expats feel that they should make the most of the situation but, at the end of the day, it makes their life tougher in meeting profit targets. Those on small housing allowances or none at all have to be more creative in finding accommodation which they consider habitable. Find a friendly real estate person to help you from the moment you arrive.

Create a place of comfort and identity
Working in China can be unbelievably stressful—there can be a feeling of ambiguity, chaos and of being distinctly outside your comfort zone. You must create a quiet, comfortable and homely retreat for yourself in which to unwind. Keep your apartment free of clutter from the office, or at least relegate office paperwork to just one room, so you can shut the door on it.

Finding a retreat away from the office can be difficult for expats working for Siemens, the major German industrial group, at their headquarters in Beijing. Since Siemens has its own housing and office complex, expat staff can actually still see their desks and in-trays from their apartment windows. 'It's too much,' complained one executive. 'I'm desperately trying to relax and think about something not connected with work after a busy week, and I look out of the window and see my in-tray. Then, before I know it, I find myself sitting at that desk again, even though it's the weekend. If I was living further away, I might be able to relax a bit more effectively!'

If you are inspecting houses during the summer, many may seem very attractive. However, don't forget China's long winters: in many parts of China, the weather conditions can be extreme for much of the year. Even new apartments (or perhaps one should say, *especially* new apartments) are prone to freezing draughts due to the poor quality of window and door fittings. Reverse-cycle air-conditioners are good in the summer months, but can be inadequate in winter; they also have a very drying effect. Look for somewhere that will be cosy and comfortable during those long winter months.

In your home, try and strike a balance between your current life in China and your background—neither break all links with the past nor hang on too much to the familiar. China souvenirs look great in China and are fun to buy, but don't go overboard. Keep some things from home. In particular, bring photos of family and friends, and of your home in your own country. Visitors will be fascinated and, more importantly, you'll have ongoing reminders of your cultural identity.

Settling in

When you start work in China, you'll find yourself far too busy to do much on the domestic front. Unless you have a partner who can take care of things while you're at the office, you'd better get set up now. If you can have a few days off before starting work, all the better—spend the time getting everything in place so that, later on, you don't have to worry and can concentrate on your work.

Settling in means finding and moving in to your apartment, acquiring furniture, hiring a domestic helper or *ayi,* and finding out where the local shops are for your basic daily requirements. One Western expatriate woman moved into an unfurnished apartment and never got around to furnishing it; another moved into a hotel and never got around to finding an apartment; another waited for monthly trips to Hong Kong for all her shopping.

Navigate the bureaucracy
Other guidebooks to living in China (see Bibliography) give more detailed information on getting your resident's card, employment card, compulsory medical examination and the multitude of other bureaucratic details which must be finalized before you are officially based in China. If you're working for a company in China, your human resources department might be able to relieve you of these details—it's a minefield for unwary Westerners to penetrate on their own. If you're not with an established company, find a Chinese-speaking and experienced friend to advise and go with you to all these Government offices.

If you meet any senior Chinese officials at cocktail parties, be very pleasant to them and make sure you get their *mingpian.* One Western expat met the head of the Aliens Exit and Entry Department at a banquet just at the time she needed her visa renewed. She was expecting to wait six weeks—she was able to get it in three after a quick telephone call to her new friend. Such *guanxi* is immeasurably useful.

If your rent is paid by your company, make sure it has all the information it needs, such as landlord's name and address, bank account number and all documentation, including the lease agreement. Much of this will be in Chinese; all the bills will be in Chinese. If you're a Westerner, instruct your staff, your human resources department or your accounts department to take care of things. Even your *ayi* can do it if you leave the money for her. As in most other countries, there are penalties for late payments of bills. If you move house, you must inform the *gong an*. They'll need to see your new and old lease contracts; take all the rest of your documentation in case it's needed.

Establish routines for a normal life
When you first arrive, everything will be so weird that you'll feel as if you're floating in time and space, that you don't even know what day of the week it is. To make your life as normal as possible, try to establish a regular routine of getting up, going to work, getting exercise, and doing the same sort of things you did at home or at your last, less unusual posting.

For example, if you used to go to the movies once a week, get a video and watch it with friends. You can't rent videos as you would elsewhere, because the distribution of foreign movies is restricted in China. However, as explained in the *Beijing Scene Guidebook*, you can tell how long expats have been in China by the size of their video collections, and friends informally exchange videos for regular viewings, especially during the winters. If you used to play sports, find a local team. They are probably desperate for new members.

Favourite foods and beverages are best brought from outside until you can find a local supplier. Your own coffee mug and desk accessories can also help to recreate a feeling of 'normalcy' in what, for several months, will be a very crazy world.

Bringing the family

Perhaps the ultimate way of showing your commitment to a life and career in China is to bring your family with you when you relocate. Jim King insists that you need the support of your family to cope with the demands and challenges of living in China, so you should bring them with you. Others leave their wives and children in their country of origin or nearby in Hong Kong—it's a matter of choice. But those with their families never regret their decision, while those without them frequently suffer loneliness and anxiety, as well as possibly deteriorating relationships. Although living in China can put stress on relationships, it is just as likely to be a bonding experience.

When **Lee Swee Chee** moved to China with his family, he already had some idea of the situation he would have to adapt to in China because he'd been covering China out of Singapore for two years before making the move. But his wife wasn't so familiarized. 'The hardest person to convince was my wife,' Lee recalls. 'It was tougher then, four years ago, with no shops really, nothing much to do; and then we had the two-currency system, with foreigners having to use FECs. It's now much easier.' (FECs, Foreign Exchange Certificates, were a separate currency which had to be used by all foreigners making purchases in China. They were abolished in 1993.)

Think of your partner's needs
Lee Swee Chee's first job on arrival was to find a suitable home, especially one that his partner liked. 'The flat must be one your wife likes,' he advises all married couples where the husband works and the wife is at home. 'She will be there more of the time than you, especially if you are travelling a lot as well as working long hours.'

Children, who tend to be more adaptable, are good at making friends at school. This can help their mothers settle in as they will meet other mothers through the children and find interesting activities. Lee also recommends joining social clubs, such as the Malaysia Club of Shanghai, which has between 700 and 800 members; he also stresses the importance of finding some relaxing activities outside the office.

Jim King comments that his wife had difficulties in finding a job in China, at first. 'Maybe the jobs she's been doing are not as good as she could get in the US, but she still feels that she is accomplishing something worthwhile.'

Partners can be more successful working freelance or setting up their own businesses, making use of expertise developed at home or in other postings. These businesses can include English or other language teaching, training in basic management skills, photography, beauty therapy, catering, freelance writing and translation—to name but a few. Beijing and Shanghai, in particular, have large expat communities who have the needs of other like-sized communities, to say nothing of the needs of the local population.

Choose a good school for your children
Then you need to find a school for your children, which, again, is much easier than it used to be, particularly in Beijing and Shanghai. **Michael Wu** worried a lot about the quality of schooling for his children in China. However, he considers that being based in a major city, such as Beijing, Shanghai or Guangzhou, has big advantages. 'Your children's education can suffer if you're not in a big city,' he points out. 'For expatriates working in out-of-the-way places, it may be better to leave your family at home, primarily for the sake of the children's education. But in Guangzhou, for example, it's OK. It's actually more like being in the New Territories of Hong Kong than being in China. The International School is good, although tuition is expensive. The same is true in Shanghai and Beijing.'

Share the adventure with your family
Jim King's wife and daughter accompanied him to China because, he says, 'We all felt that we should appreciate the hardships together, and share my conviction about China. We agreed that if it was too much, we would return to the US. But we stayed and now, six years later, it's a lot better, and we quite like it here.'

Jim King's daughter attends the Beijing International School. 'She's learning a lot about China, but she's still in touch with the US education system. Her class-mates come from all over the world. This is better than her being in school in the US.'

Families together in China can make the most of their opportunities by helping each other to learn Mandarin or Shanghainese, for example. For Western wives trying to shop and get around, it makes life much easier, and if they can help and motivate their husbands, all the better. Years down the track, back in the United States or the United Kingdom, for example, they'll still have a big collection of jokes to share, based very largely on the *faux pas* they made while learning such a difficult and ambiguous language with such opportunities for hilarious misinterpretation.

Enjoy the support of your family
Michael Wu was glad he brought his family with him. 'When I first arrived in Guangzhou, after living in Canada, I found it very tough; the first six months, in particular, were the toughest. I wasn't sure if I was going to stay: I didn't unpack my bags fully until I decided. But I had my family with me all along. This was a big advantage, to have their help and support.' The presence of his family helped him to come to terms with the massive changes and uncertainties in his work-style and life-style.

Many Hong Kong Chinese executives working in China commute into China from Hong Kong on a weekly or monthly basis, their families staying in Hong Kong. This tends to make them feel they're living in China only temporarily. Some prefer it that way, and comfort themselves with the thought that they're still really living in Hong Kong, but the drawback is that it shows, to the local staff, a lack of long-term commitment to them and to the success of the local business. There is also the personal disadvantage of the lack of family support when the executive is in China.

Having one's family around can make relaxing easier, and provides an opportunity to get away from work and go out and explore. Facilities, such as parks and gardens, are being spruced up regularly to benefit the flood of tourists now visiting China. Many people purchase bicycles and get out and about, while at other times they relax by home-building and shopping.

Those who don't bring their families often tend to become workaholics and recluses in China. How do you relax if you're on your own, without this close support and companionship? Common answers to this question are: 'I just go to the gym in the hotel and work out, then go to sleep'; 'I just lie in the bath reading the newspaper and go to sleep'; 'I go out with my colleagues from work every night'; and 'I just work all evening, grab some fast food, and go to sleep'.

Those used to being on their own, single people who've spent several years travelling, tend to be more proactive in trying to find ways to relax and enjoy being in China without a family. They're the most active in finding friends and ways of entertaining themselves.

Devise a strategy to survive separation

One Shanghai-based Taiwanese–American executive decided that his American wife, whom he met in Taiwan, would stay in Hong Kong to run her own business and complete her studies, while he moved to Shanghai. He recommends that others in this situation should make arrangements with their companies to come back to visit their partners on a regular basis. He returns to Hong Kong once a month for reporting purposes, and the company agreed to split his housing allowance between the two cities. He lives modestly in a small apartment in Shanghai, leaving the bulk of his allowance for his wife's Hong Kong home. He also gets two R&R trips out of Shanghai annually, and home leave to the United States, which can be another opportunity to see his wife. With her trips to Shanghai, they are able to see each other, on average, once every three weeks. 'It's not ideal, but it's basically workable,' he says.

Craig Pepples managed on his own for his first two years in China, before his wife joined him at the beginning of year three. 'My strategy for surviving on a personal basis was to be as self-sufficient as possible,' he says. 'I created my own "bubble world", in which I made sure that I had the things that I like, such as books and music. When so much of my outside world was out of my control, I felt I had to have something I could control, just simple things.' Pepples feels that a commuting marriage is OK for a short time—if you can see each other around every two to three weeks—but is unsatisfactory in the long term.

However, he recalls, 'It meant that, in the beginning, I didn't have a nest. I camped out, I didn't settle, and I still regarded Hong Kong as home because my wife and our home were there. It was only when she moved here with our dogs and cats and we finally gave up our home in Hong Kong, that I felt I really lived in China. This made a very big difference: I noticed it straight away. My staff also felt it—it was like they were asking themselves, "How committed is this person to being in China?" and "Is this company going to stay long term in China?" and, naturally, "How secure is my job here, given these circumstances?" When an expat manager physically moves to China, with his or her partner, the staff see this is real.'

Using local services

Part of settling in is getting acquainted with what's available in your local neighbourhood. Take advantage of anything and everything that can make your life easier.

Get an ayi to help with the housework

*Ayi*s are very useful whether you're single or married. She's usually a warm and motherly local lady who's quite happy to clean your place and your clothes (and even cook) in return for quite modest wages. She can come every day or just a few times a week, as needed. After a gruelling week, the last thing you want to do is clean and wash, especially as, in China, domestic help costs a fraction of what it would in the West. Partners will also be glad of help, especially if they are pursuing their own careers. Messages left in Chinese can give the *ayi* further instructions, if needed.

The best way for Westerners to engage domestic help is to ask Chinese-speaking staff or friends to find them an *ayi*, and then to open lines of communication between them and the *ayi* in order to pass on details of what is required.

Your *ayi* can do more than routine domestic work; she can be a godsend when you have a hectic working life, and especially when you are entertaining visitors and friends. Western expats hold many successful dinner parties in China where the cooking is done by the *ayi* (and making a very suitable impression on a visiting boss). Despite an almost total language gap, compensated for with huge amounts of very dramatic body language, great dishes can be rustled up. If an obliging local staff member can give the *ayi* instructions and details of the shopping list over the telephone, all she needs is cash and most of the day to prepare. Exclamations of delight during tasting sessions with her in the kitchen will give her great 'face'. (By the way, call her '*Ayi*'—it's a title as well as a noun.)

Use local shops and facilities

Shopping in all but the major cities of China is a great challenge. Goods tend to be stashed away on counters behind the shopkeeper, so you need to know exactly what you require, and in Chinese. A better idea is to give the job to the *ayi*, or to one's driver, especially in the interests of obtaining better prices. Shanghai and Beijing now compare well with Hong Kong, but choice is still restricted, prices are generally higher, and quality can be questionable. But, as publications such as *Beijing Scene Guidebook* point out, shopping in China is now a tolerable experience, almost entirely unrelated to the deprivations of the 1980s.

Some supermarkets will deliver food and groceries to your apartment, especially if you live in an apartment block that has many expat tenants. Beware of hotel delicatessen counters—they are usually unbelievably expensive. 'I lost weight working in China,' one Western expat commented, 'simply because I refused to pay such outrageous prices for my favourite goodies, such as cheese. One tiny slice cost about the same as a huge wedge back home, so I just bought the tiny slice and thought, "Well, I'll have to get used to less, and try to enjoy it just as much".'

Many favourite restaurants will deliver take-aways to your home. Ask them where they buy their food—this could be another source of delivered items.

Maintaining your health

Before entering China, seek specialist advice on the current recommendations for inoculation in force in different parts of the country. It is also advisable to find out the situation in places that are off the beaten track, especially if your work involves travelling around China.

Jim King maintains that you need good health to be effective in China, because it's so demanding, yet most expats find it's not that easy to stay healthy here. Lee Swee Chee of Honeywell says, 'You should make sure you always get at least one day off a week, in which you do no work and get a complete rest, otherwise you won't be able to keep going.' Getting out of China to Hong Kong and elsewhere is also extremely beneficial to reduce stress, relax, and stock up on vitamins and health foods.

Mark Gau finds that it's easy to get sick in Shanghai, where he's based, so it's important to watch personal hygiene, in particular. 'I've got into the habit of washing my face and hands every hour with disinfectant soap,' he says. 'It sounds odd, but it really works. I've become much healthier this way. And I never drink local water—I have big tubs of distilled water delivered to my apartment.'

Bring your own food supplements
You should bring your regular supplies of vitamins and food supplements with you. Prospects of purchasing them in China are not good and you're even more likely to fall ill without them. The nutritional quality of local food, especially if it has been brought in from a distance and thoroughly cooked, may not be good, and it's too dangerous to eat raw food except in very reliable establishments.

Local fruits are good, but can only be consumed at work if you have facilities for washing and preparation. Some Westerners find Chinese fruits and vegetables taste odd because of the different fertilizers and pesticides used. Also, the varieties developed for Chinese taste are not necessarily palatable to Westerners.

Exercise for good health

Craig Pepples joined a health club when he first arrived in Shanghai. 'This was a major break with habit, it wasn't something I'd ever done before. But it fitted in with being here, especially because my wife wasn't with me at first. I found that going to the gym was a chance to recalibrate myself after a stressful and perplexing day at work.'

Expats find that exercise is a great way to cope with the increased stress that working in China places on mental well-being and health. That this is a widely held view is demonstrated by the capacity crowds attracted to health clubs and gyms and the long waiting lists at both. Jogging, which draws stares of disbelief from locals, is also a good way to get around as well as get exercise, but watch for those fumes and crazy cyclists and drivers.

Be aware of pollution

Pollution in China is becoming so serious that many expats suffer respiratory ailments within a short time of arrival, suffering from such symptoms as persistent coughs, repeated colds and feeling generally run down. The good news is that you do become acclimatized fairly quickly and your health eventually returns. This is an inevitable phase and probably can't be avoided, even by the fittest. The best advice is to keep up the exercise and healthy food in order to recover quickly and ward off future perils.

Try local food, cautiously

Expats who join in and don't turn up their noses are quickly made welcome by locals. A big part of this process is eating local food, especially as this is one of the most popular occupations in China. Few local dishes are totally inedible, even for those of delicate stomachs. Even things which look and smell revolting need not be totally stomach-turning. It's best to try a little of everything and show willing, and limit yourself to a single mouthful for the really disgusting items. If the restaurant seems to be large and popular, and is clean and well air-conditioned, it should be OK hygiene-wise. Expats are just as likely to get sick in expensive five-star hotels as they are in local-but-good restaurants.

Street food is probably best avoided. This is a shame, because locals say it can be very good, but it may be just too risky for the typical expat digestive system (and this includes many overseas Chinese).

Making friends

Start making friends as soon as you can after arriving in China—and keep on making them. Your first contact will be with other people in your office, yet you should make an effort to make friends outside your work environment. Exposure to the lives and experiences of people from different backgrounds will widen your horizons and help you keep a balance between work and leisure.

One who wishes to preserve health must avoid extremes.
He must not allow himself to be too caught up in worldly entanglements
Or over-exert himself with excessive occupation.
A gentleman must embrace the troubles of both body and mind
But be steeped in the delights of wind and moon.

CAI GEN TAI(*Roots of Wisdom*) c. 1630

Learn from other cultures

'The first group of people I met were working in our joint venture, and I tended to spend time with them in the evenings,' says Mark Gau. 'To a large extent this has continued, and I do a lot of team-building with them this way. In China, I think this is very important, and I've worked hard to build trust this way. I've also gone back to my distant roots by exploring Chinese culture and art. I'm learning to play a Chinese musical instrument, and I go driving with a colleague to small villages, especially where famous Chinese artists were born. It's amazing how many talented local people there are who are willing to teach you about art or music or languages, who will charge you relatively little money.'

Many expats find that, in the smaller expat communities, they're able to meet people whose backgrounds are quite different from the backgrounds of people they meet at home. It's certainly a good form of stress release to hear other people let off steam about their frustrations, especially if their background is quite different from yours. They'll be interested in your frustrations, too. You may also find out that they are suffering much more than you are!

Try and bridge the social gap
Johnny Ho recalls that, in the early 1990s, Shanghai had few entertainment and leisure facilities compared with the situation in the last couple of years. 'There were very few places to go to after work,' he recalls. 'Also—and this is an ongoing problem—it's difficult for us, as expats, to make friends with the locals. Often, the gap is too wide. There is a big difference in our earnings, for example. You can't keep taking someone out for dinner when they can't afford to return the hospitality, and it would be rather insensitive to take them back to an expat home when theirs is much smaller and more modest—it would be embarrassing for them, if they felt they were expected to invite you back to their home.'

So Ho, like many expats, both Chinese and Western, tends to mix with other expats socially while trying to build bridges to local staff in the office and during company social events.

Exploring your locality

Maps are improving but are still difficult to come by, so finding your own way around is preferable. Good guide-books can help, especially if you're interested in local history, architecture, gardens or whatever. People-watching can be very entertaining. One Westerner was amazed to observe elderly men preparing vegetables for lunch, homing pigeons being freed and returning, baskets being woven, and clothes being hung precariously out of high-rise apartment block windows. If you start to get bored with your environment, invite a friend to come and stay for the weekend. Seeing it all again through their eyes will certainly revive your interest.

Get a bicycle or walking shoes
Riding a bicycle in China is not for the faint-hearted or for the weak-chested—it can be terrifying and certainly involves breathing in huge amounts of pollution. It's almost as treacherous to walk around, because bicycles, motor bikes and even cars frequently mount the pavements and swerve dangerously near to pedestrians. This seems to be quite legal, because the *gong an* do it, too! But cycling and walking are really the only ways to get to know your locality.

Learn to find your own way around
It's very frustrating to be dependent on staff to get around, so learn how to get to the most important places quickly and easily. When you have visitors, you can impress them with your local knowledge. Bosses will be satisfied that you've made a big effort, and may give you extra Brownie points for your adaptability. You may even come to be seen as a model expat, with possible further (and hopefully more remunerative) postings in the offing.

Cultural perspectives

Finding Chinese cultural sites is not necessarily easy, in view of the havoc wreaked upon them during the Cultural Revolution. However, Beijing has many such places, and most major cities have something of Chinese historical interest. It's all a question of feeling part of the scene. To regard the Hard Rock Cafe and the China World Hotel as the only places to go to in Beijing would definitely mark you as one of the less adventurous expats. It would be a shame to leave Beijing having never climbed the Great Wall, the Fragrant Hills or the Beihai Park temple, although it is not unheard-of.

Get to know more about Chinese culture
Chinese culture holds a fascination for all visitors, whether Westerners discovering it for the first time or overseas Chinese out of touch with their origins. But see it in the context of your own culture, and don't get carried away. Bear in mind that, particularly in Shanghai and, to a certain extent, in the Southern cities, there isn't much Chinese culture to be found—much of it was wiped out in the Cultural Revolution. The popularity of the new quasi-American culture and highly commercially oriented attitude of the rising generation means that much of the culture lies below the surface.

Two Italian executives working in Shanghai complained that there was no such thing as Chinese culture. 'There's just Macdonald's and KFC and American pop songs playing in the taxis. In Italy, we have Giotto, Michelangelo, Machiavelli, and all the great opera classics. Italian culture is much greater than Chinese culture!' They're wrong, of course, as no culture is necessarily greater than any other, but they can be forgiven for finding Chinese culture inaccessible and unavailable.

Many Westerners find much more Chinese culture in Taiwan, Hong Kong and even Singapore than they do in China, particularly in the big business cities. However, you can easily enjoy Chinese music, at the opera and the ballet, and much Chinese architecture remains. A large body of Chinese literature is available through the Chinese classics (much of it well-translated). When you open these books, don't be put off by prefaces along the lines of 'Remember this is bourgeois and decadent pre-Liberation misguided thinking'—this will be written by officials who, although they want to keep Chinese literature alive, no longer condone its values. Don't read the prefaces at all, just enjoy the books.

Beware of the tendency of Chinese to feel that their cultural heritage makes up for the failings of the present and the recent past. Everyone, even the most humble peasant, is proud of his or her country's status as 'The Middle Kingdom, half-way between Heaven and Earth'. Of course, such pride and patriotism are in many ways admirable, and many Westerners respect this characteristic, which is in contrast to a perceived lack of patriotism in other countries. However, it is this characteristic, this pride in 5000 years of history, and the long-term, dynastically oriented thinking of most Chinese, that makes the inexcusable excesses of Chairman Mao somehow acceptable.

A visiting consultant says, 'Sometimes I feel like saying to the Chinese managers, especially those propping up decaying State-owned enterprises, "What use are all the treasures of the Ming dynasty to you now?" I'm just sick of hearing about 5000 years of history. They must forget this and get on with what's happening now!'

Stay in touch with your own culture
Craig Pepples finds that, despite his love of Chinese culture and interest in the Chinese language, cultural

deprivation is one of the biggest drawbacks of living in China. 'If you watch the Chinese news on TV, it's so slanted, it's so one-sided. We used to make jokes about CNN in the US, but really the Chinese media is totally manipulated. They black out the Internet, and they put people in prison for having religious beliefs.

'You need a constant reality check to keep reminding yourself that this is not normal for you,' he continues. 'So it's good to have visitors, and to get out of China often yourself, and to have friends who have a similar background to yourself, to remind you of your roots, your values, your background, and where you're coming from.'

The mother of one China-based executive wrote to her daughter, asking, 'Can't you get another job in another country where the people are more like us?'. She had a point. To live happily in China, it's important to keep in touch with your own values and understanding, as well as build an understanding of the culture of the country where you're living.

Chapter 9

Lessons to be learnt: the expat experience

The benefits of hindsight are well-known—'If only I'd known then what I know now' is a common refrain. If you are contemplating a career move into China, then the following may well have a major influence on your ultimate decision.

Living in China and your career

Jim King advises that, for him, the advantages of living and working in China far outweigh the disadvantages. 'I always believe you should go to the country where you can make the greatest difference. China needs expertise from other countries. Why stay in your own country when you can make much more significant changes in a country like China? I try to influence my friends in the US to come out and join me. It's not an easy life here, but we can make a difference!'

Kathy Bao feels that how you perceive the advantages and disadvantages depends on your attitude to being in China. 'Do you see China as an extremely important future market which could play a very important part in the rest of your life? Or do you just want to come and take a look? If the latter is the case, then stay at home,' she says. 'China takes a long-term effort and is a long-term commitment. You can't look back. Your life changes completely—I have already gone past the point of no return. You will always have difficulties, you will always have bottle-necks, so, if you don't like this, you should give up and go home.'

Michael Wu considers that China is a great place to save money and a great place to learn. 'It's a real survival test, it makes you tough. But unless you can get out regularly and keep yourself updated about what is happening at the cutting edge of your profession in the outside world, you'll get outdated and your standards will slip. If I'm too long in China, I become too tolerant of poor quality; I also worry about the quality of my children's education.'

Mark Gau sees advantages and disadvantages to being in China, career-wise. 'I'm now somewhat type-cast as a China expert, and I'm seen to be in a regional job rather than a head office job, which would be no good if I wanted to go back to the US,' he says. 'My access to information is limited, I'm cut off from head office, my job is very demanding and time-consuming as I must be so hands-on with my staff, and I can't be with my wife so much.' However, on the positive side, Gau feels that being in China is personally challenging and gratifying, that he's learning a lot and is being forced to think all the time.

Stephen White says the biggest advantage of being in China was the opportunity to learn how to set up a business from scratch, rather than just being another employee or even a partner in a business. 'I had to know how to register the company, find an office, hire staff, open the bank accounts, do all the legal and financial stuff, all in a strange place, all on my own. It was a completely new experience for me, and it has given me a lot of confidence for doing it again, in China or elsewhere.' Many people feel that, as China is the most difficult place in the world to do business, success there virtually guarantees success elsewhere.

Simon Aliband considers that to be successful in China you have to devote a tremendous amount of your time to your work, while the amount of time left for yourself is limited. On the other hand, it is very exciting to be part of the new China, particularly in Shanghai, which is now experiencing such a renaissance. 'Life is definitely harder here, even if you can speak Chinese fluently. I always think that if I can run an office with 20 Chinese, then running an office in England would be so easy!'

Irene Wolinski, originally from Taiwan, finds that after a long career in the United States, she still finds herself more accepted back in China. 'I never really settled in the US, I never felt quite at home. I'm actually more at home here in China where I look like everyone else, although

I'm actually now quite American in my outlook. But with my American experience and my senior position in a US multinational, I have a much better standard of living than most Chinese; I'm living like an American expat, not like a Chinese at all.'

Craig Pepples identifies other career advantages, those of working in a market '...where the potential for future growth is obvious, although there's always a risk that something so volatile could go bad. However, the twenty-first century will be China's, and those of us here already are getting a head start in getting to grips with this strange place'. Also, as we saw above, being in China can give an executive the opportunity to set up a whole operation, to be a general manager in the true sense of the word, to get experience of running an entire operation.

Pepples also talks about the dangers of being seen as 'Mr China'. 'I'm finding myself painted into a corner. Perhaps it's partly my language ability—because I speak Chinese, it's logical for me to be here, especially because China is seen as so different, so impenetrable. This view is definitely fostered by the locals. Other senior executives in our company who speak no Asian languages spend their time zapping all around Asia setting up and running businesses, moving from country to country. With my experience, maybe I could be seen in the context of "Mr Emerging Markets". But I've got into the mould of China. I try to argue that China should be seen in the context of the rest of the world, and I try to watch this "Mr China" syndrome. "Mr China" people are either orientalist Westerners like myself, or people who may be very Western but who happen to look Chinese.

'Either way, it's easy to be type-cast, which can restrict future career moves. Another danger is that being so focused on China for such a long time means you're like an ostrich with its head in the sand. You can't see what's around you, and you inevitably go around accusing others that they don't know China. You become very inward-looking, and you can become so fascinated with China that there's a real danger that you will never leave. My chairman used to describe China as "a black hole"; in a sense, he was right. People get sucked into China and are never seen again.'

David Kutena shares some of these views. He doesn't speak Chinese and, although he's interested in working in China as a long-term commitment, he is also worried about the effects on his future career. An Australian working in a German company, he bemoans the fact that many of the upwardly mobile Germans in head office won't come to China. He says, 'They're afraid they'll be out of the mainstream, that it will side-track them from going to the top in the organization. Maybe two or, at the most, three years in China is OK, but any longer than that is really dangerous. They've been told that in 10 to 15 years' time, they'll be in the running for a very serious job with all the perks, and they don't want to risk that. This is to say nothing of the disadvantages they see to their personal lives, and the fact that their partners mostly wouldn't like to come.'

This may be a new syndrome, the perception that expatriates in China may actually be a different breed than expatriates in other countries or head office people generally. If they are a different breed, they may not fit in with the corporate culture of head office and may also be unable to establish that culture in China, something which would—and does—cause a new set of problems. Companies with extensive numbers of expats in the field may need to offer assurances of future career opportunities at the heart of the company in order to attract committed company people to jobs on the periphery for parts of their careers. The alternative, of hiring a new breed of long-term expat who doubt they will be able to, or will be offered the opportunity to, return to a senior position in the company heartland, may lead to diluted cultures, too much autonomy of local operations and a failure to build synergies with the rest of the global organization. Why are multinational companies coming to China? When hiring senior staff for subsidiaries on the periphery, especially in China, the recruitment policy adopted should be based on the company's reasons for being there.

Personal experiences of living in China

Based on the personal experiences of the author over nearly two years, and the personal experiences of many China-based expatriates living and working in China who were interviewed for this book, it's possible to summarize the range of emotions and feelings that a China posting can evoke.

On the positive side, there's amazement and incredulity, friendship and warmth, helpfulness, the widening of horizons, experience of a different culture, excitement, opportunities for adventure, a lack of boredom, opportunities for achievements, and opportunities to make a contribution. The following stories illustrate two of these positive aspects.

The first story shows the helpfulness of people in China.

'One day, in June 1996, during the rainy season in Shanghai, it was raining so heavily that around the entrance to our office the water was around three feet deep. It was almost impossible to get out, without getting very wet and very dirty, because all sorts of rubbish was floating around in the smelly brown "river" washing the sides of our building and the old nineteenth-century ladies' college next to it. Watermelon peelings, eggshells, discarded polystyrene lunch-boxes and other detritus bobbed around in the water while my staff and I peered out, wondering how we were going to get to the little restaurant across the street where we went for our weekly staff lunch.

'Then, suddenly, cheerily whistling, appeared a cyclist, not on a conventional bicycle but on a three-wheeled cart-cum-bicycle. As he pedalled, his feet regularly disappeared under the brown tide, as the water lapped more than half-way up his wheels, but the small cart behind him was just above the water-line. Without being asked, he backed up to our step and invited us to climb aboard. "Does he work in our office? Does anyone know him?", I asked, but "no".

'Some of the girls were screaming and all were clutching each other as the cart lurched when the unknown cyclist started struggling to pedal half under water. But we arrived at our restaurant steps, dry and clean, although beginning to worry how we'd get back again. Everyone shouted *xie xie ni* [thank you] and *feichang xie xie ni* [thank you very much] as the helpful cyclist pedalled off to find more stranded people.'

The second story illustrates the kind of amazement you will feel.

'It was the last day of Chinese New Year, and there was a lantern festival at the Yu Gardens in Shanghai. The crowd was so dense, it was like the whole population of 16 to 18 million people had turned out all at once to witness this happy family occasion, where children carried home-made lanterns made from paper and candles, or bought garishly coloured plastic ones with torch-sized light-bulbs inside.

'The tea-house in the middle of the lake, unable to cope with such a huge throng of customers, had given up trying to serve its traditional bean curd strips, tiny pigeon's eggs and rice wrapped in lotus leaves, and instead was giving out boxes of different-flavoured jellies, pre-packaged like airline food.

'I was with a friend and two other people, and we knew that the biggest problem would be the possibility of losing each other in the crowd. As expected, this happened, and we wondered how on earth we would find our friends, as the Shanghai police pushed and shoved the heaving crowd squashing itself around the famous zig-zag bridge. We called out for them, but the noise of everyone around was so loud that they had no chance of hearing us.

'Then I had an idea, the mobile telephone! I quickly tapped out my friend's number—almost all business people and managers have mobiles in Shanghai, it must be the most densely penetrated market in China—and I could then hear him saying, "I'm right next to the start of the bridge", which was exactly where I was. Then, only about 10 yards away, I could just make out his arm waving above the mass of people. It had been so crowded that even 10 yards away I couldn't see him and I couldn't hear his mobile ringing. Despite living in London and visiting cities like New York and Tokyo, I've never seen such an amazingly large crowd of people in my life.'

The negative aspects of living in China can bring feelings of frustration and irritation, anger and annoyance, discomfort and chaos, ambiguity, and shock and disgust. You are likely to suffer from misunderstandings and feel you lack control over your life. Stories like the following are not uncommon.

The first story illustrates the frustration and irritation you can sometimes feel in China.

'I was on a bus in Beijing, heading out for the Fragrant Hills with a friend for a day's walking. We knew that it would be quite a long journey, and we were looking forward to getting to our destination as quickly as possible, so we could start our walk, hoping that the lovely summer weather would not turn to rain.

'The bus was a small local one, with around 16 seats, occupied by a variety of people, housewives and workers. Most people were fairly good-natured, but began to get a bit fed up as the conductor of the bus asked the bus driver to stop at every stop for at least five minutes while he tried to get more passengers on. It was clearly turning out to be an unproductive exercise and the existing passengers began to leave the bus, irritated that their journey was taking so long. The new passengers persuaded to get on were soon far outnumbered by those departing, and soon we got off the bus, too, despite having paid full fare all the way to our destination, because this bus conductor was spending so much time soliciting for business that it would be hours before we got to our destination!'

The next story illustrates the anger and annoyance that can be experienced in China.

'We booked a room in a hotel for a function, a public seminar. One of our problems with using hotels in China is that often there's another function next door which can be very noisy and disturbs us, causing our customers to complain. So we asked the hotel if the room next to ours was booked and, if so, would it be a particularly noisy function? They said it wasn't booked at all, that it would be free. In retrospect, they may have said that through fear that we might cancel our booking. Then, when we'd started our function, suddenly all these people turned up from a software company to have a very noisy multimedia event right next door.

'I spoke to the organizer [of the software company event] and discovered that she'd had exactly the same experience. She had asked the hotel to make sure that there wasn't a booking in the room next door that might be disturbed by the software company because she knew how noisy it would be! We came to the conclusion that not only did the hotel not want to lose our bookings, but may not even have bothered to look at the bookings list. The staff of the hotel have a tendency to tell customers what they think they want to hear, regardless of whether this is the truth or not! It was very annoying. And now you don't know whether to believe them or not.'

A survey on the expat experience

Further insights into the nature of the experience of expats working and living in China are provided by the results of a survey conducted in 1996 by the China Research Unit of Manchester Business School in the United Kingdom, as part of a project for the European Commission on the training needs of expatriates in China. The subsequent report was published in August 1996.

Survey companies, and focus
The survey excluded overseas Chinese and expatriates working for other than European companies, but included detailed feedback from 65 expats from 53 companies. These companies include some famous names who have made a major commitment to the China market over the last decade, and who employ very large numbers of both expats and locals. They are ABB, Alcatel, BASF, BP, Citroen, Ericsson, Heineken, Jebsen, Lufthansa, Philips, Price Waterhouse, Reuters, Roche, Siemens, Thomson CSF and Xian-Janssen.

According to faculty members at Manchester Business School, 'While most companies have a small number of expatriates, a few have tens and even hundreds. Over the next three years, the number of expatriates will increase, but not as rapidly as over the last three years [ie, 1993–96]'. So the survey sees an ongoing need for expats to continue coming to China and working here, but recognizes that localization will become more and more significant.

The survey questionnaire completed by each expat covered such areas as the nature of the expat's current assignment in China in the context of their careers as a whole; how they were selected and recruited for the assignment; how they (and their partners, if relevant) were prepared before departure; their current and ongoing training needs in China; their opinion of the requirements for expatriate effectiveness; and company and personal profiles.

Younger managers find it hard going
Nigel Campbell and Howard Ward of Manchester Business School, and Tim McNeill of Euroventures, a venture capital firm advising on the report, make a number of key points in it. 'Over 25 per cent of expatriates are experiencing considerable difficulties. This is the average opinion of managers in the survey. Younger managers believe that the figure is over 45 per cent.' This would indicate that, although many expats experience problems, the younger expats in particular find life tougher.

Perhaps the higher figure for younger managers might be explained by the tendency of older managers to be more patient. Working in China is, above all, a severe test of patience, and those champing at the bit to make rapid progress might find China just too frustrating. This is despite the generally good facilities offered by European companies (compared with those offered by many overseas Chinese and local businesses), especially the larger operations.

The challenges for expat managers

These researchers discovered that, 'At work, the main challenges facing expatriates are developing relationships (*guanxi*), motivating, retaining and developing local staff and dealing with government bureaucracy and regulations'. Many expats find these tasks quite different from those encountered in Europe. The kind of relationships needed to get things done are different from those needed in Europe and, in any case, all expats have to build their relationships from scratch, in contrast with locals who have been busy acquiring their *guanxi* since their youth (and many were born with networks handed down from parents and other relatives). When living in China, foreigners find that the old boy network, the *Grand Ecole* system and other European inventions exist to only a limited degree—experience in the PRC is a great leveller and these European rituals count for comparatively little here.

Working with local staff poses huge problems for expats because the kind of staff problems that exist in the PRC do not exist in Europe. Staff in Europe have largely not been affected by an iron rice bowl system; they are much less mobile in terms of hopping from one job to the next, and their education has been much more practical and vocational than is the case in China. So all expats have to adapt their thinking towards local staff, and relearn their assumptions about approaches to effective management and supervision.

Similarly, the nature of the China Government's bureaucracy and regulations is (at least initially) beyond the ken of most expats, who must rely heavily on local advisers. It's difficult enough learning the existing regulations—even

PRC nationals find it extremely challenging to keep up-to-date with all the new ones. Some managers have relatively few dealings with the bureaucracy; others find that it dominates their lives. Those in the latter category point to the excessive stress that is generated, exacerbated by a feeling of being unable to control events.

Why expats are effective

The survey indeed discovered that, 'Expatriates believe that effectiveness stems from the ability to cope with stress, interpersonal skills, an adaptable family and personality factors'. Obviously, stress levels can be much higher than at home in Europe, when one considers the unfamiliarity, chaos and lack of control. The need to get on with other people, be they staff, colleagues, customers, suppliers or bosses, is also greater. In China, so much more explanation, training, coaching, support, advising and sharing is needed than in one's own country. Plus, all this is accompanied by the struggle, in a difficult environment, to maintain the quality standards espoused by head office, to build a corporate culture, to make money and to contain costs. For married expatriates, the support of their families can be key; conversely, problems within the family will always have a negative effect on the expat's performance and level of commitment.

As the survey comments, 'These personal attributes [the ability to cope with stress, interpersonal skills, an adaptable family and personality factors] were rated more highly than previous Asian experience, previous job ratings, above-average intelligence or the ability to speak Mandarin fluently'. This suggests that working and living in China is very different from elsewhere for expats in

Asia (particularly Hong Kong and Singapore), probably because of the emerging nature of the economy and the still-small expat community. Therefore, an expat's performance in a previous posting may not have much bearing on how they get on in China, especially if their job requires considerable business development work and negotiation of deals, which in China can be more problematic than in many other emerging markets.

The importance of a well-rounded personality in preference to above-average intelligence for the China-based expat is probably not a surprising finding. Very intelligent people often find it very difficult to be patient and to tolerate frustrating situations. The limitations of a relatively poor infrastructure, such as occasional power shortages, contrive to damage and incapacitate high-tech equipment upon which advanced research is usually based. Those studying advanced scientific matters, those dependent on research materials and access to libraries around the world, and those seeking to prepare excellent high-tech presentations may find themselves in one of the worst countries in the world to pursue their studies and achieve their objectives.

Very smart expats working in China may become exasperated by what they see as stupidity and dim-wittedness around them, they may lack sympathy for others and feel that progress is too slow and piecemeal. They may lack the ability to communicate on the same level as those around them and so can begin to feel isolated; they may be much less successful than a more happy-go-lucky type who takes a positive approach, even if he or she is intellectually inferior.

Mandarin, to speak or not to speak

The advantages and disadvantages of being able to speak Mandarin are the subject of much discussion among expats. Those with just a few words gape enviously at colleagues who rattle on fluently to local staff, customers and suppliers, although often these non-Mandarin speakers are greeted with much warmth by staff anxious to improve their English, who insist that their needs are much more important than his or her need to speak Chinese.

While some overseas Chinese and fluent Mandarin-speaking Westerners wonder how their inarticulate colleagues are able to survive in China, and worry that unscrupulous staff are able to take advantage of them, other expats fluent in the local tongue feel that their situation is worsened in that they get dragged into petty arguments and jealousies that they might be able to avoid if they simply didn't know what was going on. One Hong Kong Chinese expat who found herself involved in a protracted argument with a taxi driver who drove in the wrong direction reflected that if she couldn't have spoken the language, she would have just walked away. As it was, she spent several minutes in a slanging-match which ended up with the police being brought in and much-increased stress levels all round.

The survey found that, of the expats questioned, 'Fourteen of the managers, mostly the younger ones, spoke Mandarin well enough to use in business. They spoke highly of what their language skills had enabled them to achieve, but they did not rate their own performance higher than non-Mandarin speakers'. Why should this be the case? Possibly because the official language of many multinationals in China is English (and certainly not Chinese), important meetings are in most cases conducted in English, and staff are now becoming increasingly proficient in the language. English is rapidly becoming the lingua franca of the well-educated and fashionable young people in China today.

It used to be that to speak English with an American accent was highly prized; now the accents of one's boss or mentor are emulated. Local staff working in Shanghai for a French boss have even been heard to drop the 'h' in 'Shanghai', pronouncing it 'Shang-ai' in the French style, in a somewhat affected imitation of their expat manager.

In some respects, non-Mandarin speaking expats can be more successful in staff training and in understanding all the processes at work in their jobs. Where language commonality is not 100 per cent, there is more of a tendency to write everything down, to make very clear definitions, to spell everything out, to prepare descriptions and checklists, to seek clear agreement on what everything means and to overcome ambiguity. Especially in the China context, where local staff tend to avoid responsibility (particularly when they're not quite certain exactly what they will be responsible for), such a clearly documented approach to management works well and is strongly recommended by experienced China expat managers.

Selection and preparation for a China job
The survey reports that, 'Overall, managers thought they were carefully selected. Traditional recruitment methods were used (application forms and interviews). Partners were involved in the selection in half the cases'. The

survey added that, 'Preparation [for the job in China] was poor. Just over one-third of managers received no preparation at all; less than half had a preparation visit. Only five wives received any language training before departure'. When a whole family is uprooting and moving to a new environment as challenging as China, the more that they are involved, the better. If the other family members feel that the company cares about them, too, it helps in making the new assignment successful.

As we have seen earlier, having an adaptable family is cited as one of the key reasons for expat effectiveness in China. For partners, being involved in the decision to move to China, going on the preparatory visit and also receiving some preliminary language training will help them adapt.

Making a preparatory visit to China is extremely important: those who have succeeded in the PRC are often those who made several visits before moving to China to live. Moving directly from an advanced Western society to China is widely seen as being most challenging; to have spent a year or so in Hong Kong, Singapore or Taipei before beginning one's China experience is regarded as far preferable.

Support for the China expat

The survey revealed that, 'Ongoing support [for the expat in China] varied considerably. About 40 per cent of managers felt that their superiors and colleagues had a poor understanding of business in China'. This comment emphasizes the importance of education for colleagues and bosses at head office, both in the requirements of the

China-based expat and in realistic expectations. Life for most China expats would be much easier if their bosses realized the difficulties they face, and consequently the kind of understanding they need and the results they can be expected to achieve. One of the most commonly voiced complaints from expats was that their boss does not understand their circumstances.

This is an issue for both sides—the expat must keep up the information and communication flow, and the boss must make time to develop an appreciation of the demands of the China environment, not just through the occasional visit but through regular discussions and two-way feedback.

Still a hardship posting

The survey concluded that, 'Generally, China is not perceived as a desirable posting, or one which enhances career prospects'. Those about to embark on their China adventure, as we discussed at the beginning of this book, must be very clear about their reasons for taking up this challenge and be mindful of the difficulties. As discussed in this chapter, many China expats worry about their future career, the prospects for them back at head office at the end of their China stint, and the extent to which they may be labelled "Mr China" or "Ms China" and forever banished to the Middle Kingdom.

Many of those with well-paid and/or responsible jobs in China feel that they can enjoy their situation because so few are prepared to come here. Others regard themselves as 'mavericks' or certainly as people out of the corporate career track—they like project-based work and adventure and are not necessarily interested in a senior post at head office. Many actually enjoy China because it's so far away and it's so difficult for headquarters to communicate with them! If, however, you do want to safeguard your position on the ladder and are 'making a sacrifice' and coming to China in the hope that it will enhance your career prospects, you'd better get those prospects clearly identified—and, ideally, in writing—before you leave.

Localization is the way forward
The survey summary states, 'Human resources needs [of companies in China] are best met by recruiting and training local staff rather than bringing in more Westerners or overseas Chinese'. This reflects the opinion of the majority of expats surveyed. All agreed that localization is the only really cost-effective way, and the most appropriate way, of running an operation in China (as it would be in most places). However, as the survey points out, there's an ongoing need for expats for some years to come. Expats are needed to train and develop local staff; to motivate staff and help them focus on achieving the mission of the company or department; and to gradually get them used to taking more and more responsibility, and to build up judgement and decision-making skills.

It takes time to help local staff members understand how to prioritize jobs, and to know which decisions they can make on their own and which should still be made in consultation with a higher authority. For example, one local staff member made a long-distance call, during a sales call on a customer, to ask her expat boss if she should pay for lunch for the customer's wife, who happened to be there unexpectedly. A few days earlier, this same local staff member had turned down a request from a more junior member of staff, who had been with the company for over a year, to be transferred from a part-time to a full-time position—and hadn't even told her boss that this conversation had occurred. Training in such judgement calls cannot be achieved overnight, and it's arguably slower in China than elsewhere.

So the expats surveyed pointed to the ongoing help they need in this job of localization: resources and support from head office; a long-term commitment to the China market in order to maintain confidence and send a message of stability to local staff; and a feeling that China is part of the mainstream of their company's mission. Companies that have achieved a high degree of localization have done so by building a powerful corporate culture, which takes a major investment by head office in time and money.

Recommendations

The Manchester survey concluded as follows. 'Many companies are very professional in managing their expatriates. Others know what needs to be done, but find that the demands of doing business in China prevent them from doing the job as well as they would like'. So, in order to achieve an overall improvement in the experiences of China expats (remember that the survey found that over 45 per cent of China expats were suffering from various 'difficulties'), the China Research Unit made certain recommendations. Their advice was that companies operating in China should:

- Provide training for expatriates' superiors and colleagues so that they understand China business better.

- Ensure adequate opportunities for expatriates to get feedback on their performance and to discuss the problems they are experiencing.
- Pay close attention to personal attributes when recruiting expatriates.
- Involve expatriates' partners in the selection process.
- Make China postings more attractive, if their managers' current opinions are negative.
- Tap into the expanding pool of young Europeans with language skills, willing to work in China on 'local' expatriate packages. The debate will continue about the importance of language skills, but companies can benefit from recruiting from this expanding part of the labour market.
- Provide more preparation, including training in understanding Chinese business culture. Asian experience and/or experience of working on China business is helpful, but not a substitute for formal preparation for living and working in China.
- Consider sending expatriates on short courses in China about six months after the posting starts to help overcome culture shock.
- Provide language training for partners.

Those expats who feel relatively hard done by may be able to use this list of recommendations and the findings of the Manchester survey to argue for an improved level of understanding of their situation in China. In many cases, comments on their circumstances by China expats are regarded by those on the receiving end at head office as no more than a series of complaints and gripes; head office may be more convinced by the results of a more scientific survey such as that conducted by the China Research Unit.

A Different World: some cautionary tales

Overall, despite extensive modernization and opening up to the West, China remains a different world, especially in terms of infrastructural deficiencies, the extent of Government involvement and the bureaucratic nature of the regulatory environment. Here are just four, greatly simplified, examples.

Opening a bank account
The procedure involved in opening a bank account for your company at the Bank of China is typical of the extensive bureaucracy surrounding normally simple routines, and must be tolerated with good grace. It is pointless to criticize its long-windedness and even more pointless to compare it to procedures in other countries.

Quite different procedures are required for wholly foreign-owned enterprises, for joint ventures, for representative offices and for local companies. Let's look at how to open an account for a representative office, as they are among the most common form of foreign company establishment in the PRC.

First, find a friendly bank manager, preferably one introduced by a mutual friend—as in most things, it rarely works to go in cold. One way is to get to know the financial manager of the hotel where you're staying, and ask them for a recommendation and introduction. The hotel may have a branch of a bank on the premises, and if your office is located in the hotel, this makes even more sense.

You must show your registration certificate, with evidence of the name of the company and its chief representative, the nature of your scope of business, the name of the holding company or head office, the address of the head office overseas, the home address of the chief representative and the dates of his or her residence in China. Copies of all this must be left with your new bank manager. You also need a copy of your approval to do business in China from the Foreign Economic Trade Committee, and a copy of the chief representative's foreigner's registration card.

Once you have been accepted as a customer—and remember that they are doing you a favour, and not vice versa—you should immediately place a minimum of RMB 10,000 into the account (if it's a Renminbi account). If you are opening a US dollar account, then US$2000 must be deposited and the requisite forms to deposit the money completed. US dollar cash deposits are subject to three per cent bank charges, and US dollar withdrawals are subject to 0.5 per cent bank charges, based on each transaction.

Once you have deposited your Renminbi and then want to make a withdrawal in Renminbi, if it's more than RMB 10,000, you must explain why you want the money, even if you have much more than that in your account. No, you can't just ask to take your own money out again without an acceptable explanation. The reason behind this is mainly a tax issue: the authorities don't want you buying things for cash without adhering to the correct procedures and without the correct documentation. The Government is also trying to encourage the use of cheques for amounts over RMB 100 in order to reduce fraud; it also encourages bank transfers for large amounts. However, bank transfers (or TTs) take around a week for processing.

Unless you're banking at a big central bank, you must allow at least one day of processing for a withdrawal, so apply at least one day in advance. This will not suit those who like to make big ticket impulse buys—it will at least considerably curb this habit! Every afternoon, the branches send their money to the big central banks.

Also remember that you should go to the same branch of the same bank to withdraw your money, because inter-branch banking and computerized banking systems are still not widespread in the PRC. Telephone banking and other such conveniences are almost totally unknown, although ATMs are appearing on the scene in Beijing, where there are more than 30.

Savings accounts are becoming more popular in China, but don't get too excited, because the rate of interest at the time of research (mid-1996) was only 1.65 per cent per month on Renminbi accounts, and 1.57 per cent per year on US dollar accounts. These rates are not fixed and can vary from month to month. Credit cards are allowed to PRC nationals only, and have to be guaranteed to the tune of RMB 30,000 if the person works in a local work unit, ie, in a State-owned enterprise. In order to apply for a credit card, the applicant must present his or her identity card and a certificate from the personnel department of the work unit with its correct stamp. Credit cards are still very rare in China; more common are debit cards, but the processing of each transaction is very time-consuming.

At the end of the day, China is still a highly cash-based society with around 95 per cent of all transactions done in cash. Given the complications and delays inherent in the banking system, it's not surprising. Also not surprising is the fact that the paper money in circulation is often in a very poor state—dirty, torn, thin and ragged around the edges and a potential danger to health—and there's a lot of it, with the highest denomination note being RMB 100. The Government is still resisting the introduction of a RMB 500 note, fearing that it would fuel inflation and encourage forgery; it also argues that most people in China will never in their lives have so much money at one time and so will never need more than a RMB 100 note.

The number of people in China with a bank account therefore remains small, and they're nearly all companies since all companies in China must have a bank account. Individuals receive their salaries in cash, but the company keeps a sort of bank account for each person which pays interest if they do not withdraw all of their monthly cash. At each bank branch, there is a pigeon-hole for each customer, who is provided with a key to it. Into this pigeon-hole is posted all the customer's transaction information in the form of monthly statements, so it's no good waiting for it to come in the mail!

Installing a telephone switchboard

Ordering and taking delivery of one telephone line is in itself difficult enough, but trying to arrange a number of different lines linked to one main number presents difficulties of giant proportions. To have, for example, one number with 10 lines means an outlay of several thousand US dollars and a wait of up to six months, particularly in Beijing. That's why many name-cards carry several telephone and fax numbers, all of which seem to be engaged all the time. It's also a reason why many companies use hotel suites for extended periods—they have already invested the money and time to gain several telephone lines related to one number.

The very fact that it is difficult to set up a switchboard in China can be a very useful way of assessing how established a business is, its size, its *guanxi* and its commitment to the China market. If it has a switchboard, you're looking at a company which has overcome a major hurdle in China.

Purchasing a bicycle

All bicycles must be registered, insured and have an allocated parking space. The task of legally acquiring this two-wheeled contraption can take an entire day, if not longer. First, a bicycle shop must be located, the bicycle purchased and the *fapiao* issued. This must then be taken to the registration authorities before you can take possession of your bike—the owner is presented with a small metal plaque bearing the bicycle's registration details, which must be fixed to the said contraption; a certificate of registration and an insurance policy are also issued. Then it is necessary to apply for a parking space for which one pays a rental (albeit modest). The bicycle's documents are all neatly packed together in a little plastic wallet, and the owner is warned of the large expense and big *mafan* which can occur if this is lost.

But losing the documents is not nearly as likely as losing the bike itself. It is very frustrating if, after all these lengthy procedures and after such an elaborate protocol, the bicycle is stolen. Unfortunately, this is a very common occurrence. In fact, the newer and more attractive the bike, the higher the odds that your time as its owner will be very short. Despite the extensive registration and insurance procedures, the chances of seeing your bike again are extremely slim.

Becoming a dog-owner

According to the *Beijing Scene Guidebook*, only 24 breeds of dog are allowed in China (particularly in Beijing—Shanghai is a little more liberal), and they are all less than 35 cm in height. The most popular breeds are Pekingese, Chihuahua, Pomeranian and small terriers. All dogs must be registered, and sometimes the application to register a dog must be shown before the dog is purchased. The application for a dog licence can be made at the Visa Office for Foreigners and the following documents are required: the owner's residence permit, and the quarantine certificate issued at the port of entry (if you're bringing your dog in to the country) or the receipt you obtained on purchasing the animal. Processing and approval can take around 10 days. In Beijing, there's just one single licensed veterinary clinic for injections and vaccinations. Rabies injections are required twice a year. This clinic will provide a 'dog immunization certificate', which should be presented, along with three one-inch photos in colour of your dog's head, at the Visa Office, with payment for personal injury insurance and a registration fee.

Life after China

As discussed at the beginning of this chapter, there can very real career disadvantages for the long-term China executive (long-term being defined as more than three years). You should be aware of these potential problems and plan your career now. It's no good saying, 'Oh, I'll only be in China for a year or so'. Sitting at their desks in China-based companies are thousands of Western and overseas Chinese managers who came to China for a few months and stayed for half a decade or more. Ask yourself these questions, ideally before you come to China.

- Is there a job for me in head office when I want to leave China?
- Is there a job for me in my company in any other country?
- Is there a job for me in another company where they need expertise on China?
- What are my ambitions over the next five years?
- Will I just try to earn as much money as possible and then leave China?
- Will I become a 'China bore' and be unemployable if/when I return home?

If you know any people who spent several years working in executive positions in China and then left, ask them the following questions:

- Were they able to successfully integrate back into life at home?
- Were they able to successfully move to a third country?
- Were they able to get a job afterwards?
- Were they able to get over their experiences in China—were they able to stop talking about the country and were they able to have a normal life again?

However, such people are rare. China executives with long experience of China are mostly still in China, where economic opportunities are now at their greatest.

Glossary of Chinese words

The words listed below are not necessarily ordinary Chinese words with their English translations; they are words that may have other meanings, not always readily understood by the Westerner or others unfamilar with Mandarin. Even those who know Mandarin well may not realize the full implications of the use of these words in China. Understanding these words alone gives one a glimpse into Chinese thinking.

Ayi   In one context, a woman who helps around the home doing washing and cooking, but often applied to all older women as a sign of respect.

Bu dui   This means 'wrong' or, literally, 'not right'. This concept is often expressed as *dui bu dui?* or 'Right, not right?' in much the same way as 'OK?' queries acceptability. The system of verb–negative verb is very popular; *hao bu hao?* means 'Good, not good?' and *you mei you?* means 'Have, not have?'

Glossary of Chinese words

Bu ke qi   This literally means 'Don't be too polite', but really means 'You're welcome', ie, you don't need to be so polite because we don't mind helping you; however, it's in keeping with the Chinese tendency towards excessive politeness and deference.

Bu yao   Literally, 'don't want'. A very useful phrase for the tourist who is constantly being offered undesirable merchandise at rather high prices. Not actually regarded as a rude response, especially when said with a smile and suffixed with *xie xie* or 'Thank you'.

Cha bu duo

A phrase meaning 'almost' or 'just about' which is used, probably too frequently, when accepting slightly substandard goods or services instead of making an effort to bring about improvement—the bane of the lives of those trying to improve quality.

Chi fan le ma?

Literally, 'Have you eaten?'. Really, just a polite greeting, though it shows the importance of food to the average Chinese.

Dian   The Chinese word for electricity features in the Chinese names for many modern appliances, and gives an insight into the highly descriptive nature of many Chinese words, as well as how words for new concepts are created. For example, *dian hua* means 'telephone' (literally, 'electric speaking'); *dian shi* means 'television' (literally, 'electric watching'); *dian ying* means 'cinema film' or 'movie' (literally, 'electric shadows'); *dian nao* means 'computer' or 'electric brain'; and *dian ti* means 'elevator' or 'electric ladder'.

Dui bu dui?

A phrase akin to the English 'OK?' (see *Bu dui* above)

Fapiao   A receipt for goods or services, which must be numbered and must bear a 'chop' or circular stamp from the vendor. Must be obtained in order to claim back expenses, and for tax purposes. A cash register receipt, credit card docket or anything else is just not good enough. Talking about chops, make sure you get one on your air-ticket sticker if you change your flight, otherwise you will be sent to the back of a very long queue and may miss your flight.

Gong An   The police, or literally 'public peace', which gives an idea of their main focus of activities.

Guanxi   There is no exact translation into English of this very popular Chinese concept of 'relationships' with people who can help you. *Guanxi* is at the heart of your success in business dealings, in getting things done on a daily basis, and in surviving. Thus *mei you guanxi* and *mei guanxi* (literally, 'don't have relationships' and 'no relationships') mean 'it doesn't matter'.

Gweilo   The common word in Cantonese for 'foreigner' (the Mandarin word is *laowei*). A slightly perjorative term which provokes amusement when used by a foreigner to describe himself or herself in Hong Kong.

Hukou   The internal passport system common in China which deliberately prevents and slows internal migration, which is mostly to the major cities. Someone with a Beijing *houkou* would prize it highly and would not want to give it up.

Jintian   This means 'today' (not as popularly used as *mingtian* 'tomorrow', which is widely seen as a much better time to do anything).

Jiu yang da ming
    This phrase means 'Your reputation precedes you', a very formal greeting to someone you have heard of and is quite well-known but whom you've never met before; very polite and good for building your *guanxi*.

Ke yi   'OK', in the context of 'I give you permission' or 'It is allowed', rather than 'I am fine' or 'Everything is good'.

Laowei   The Mandarin word for 'foreigner'. Unlike the Cantonese word *gweilo*, this word is quite neutral. Another Mandarin term with the same meaning is *weiguo ren*.

Ma ma hu hu
    'Not good, not bad', an extremely useful expression which also shows you off as an Old China Hand the moment you use it.

Mafan   Literally, 'trouble', a useful word if you're in a difficult situation, and clearer than *wenti*, which can mean 'problem' or 'question'. *Mafan* is also very effective in the polite form

251

of *mafan nin*, 'I'm sorry to trouble you', or 'I'm sorry to disturb you', which can be impressively employed at the beginning of each request and when you begin a telephone conversation.

Mafan nin   See *Mafan*.

Maidan   Cantonese for 'the bill' in a restaurant or hotel, commonly used across China, especially in Shanghai.

Meiyou   Literally, 'We haven't got', but often used in the context of 'We don't want to serve you', 'We can't be bothered to go and fetch what you want', etc. (The book *The Man With The Key Is Not Here*, listed in the Bibliography, makes interesting reading on this subject.)

Mingpian   The name-card which everyone must have, with your name in English and Chinese, and which should be presented in both hands with a slight bow. If you haven't got a *mingpian*, you may as well stay at home, because you hardly exist without it. Foreigners should spend some time finding an acceptable Chinese name which sounds like their name when it is spoken and which also has a meaning that can be lived with. No more than four characters, unless you want to sound like a court official from the Ming dynasty.

Ni hao   Literally, 'You good?' widely used as 'Hello' and as a polite greeting. Acceptable at any time of the day or night, unlike the vaguely equivalent Cantonese form *zhou san*, which should only be used before lunch-time (because it means 'Have you had your lunch yet?', one of the most important concerns of any Chinese person).

Ta bu zai   Literally, 'He or she is out' or 'I don't know whether they're in or not, but I can't be bothered to look for you'. (Again, the book *The Man With The Key Is Not Here*, listed in the Bibliography, makes interesting reading.)

Tongzhi   Literally, 'comrade', a common greeting during the Cultural Revolution, and now rather outdated, but one which is still frequently used in textbooks teaching foreigners Chinese. It is often assumed by foreigners that Chinese deliberately teach them outdated and slightly ridiculous phrases in order to gain amusement at their expense. (This accusation is also levelled at French teachers of English.)

252

Waiguoren A Mandarin word for 'foreigner'.

Wenti A word meaning 'problem' or 'question' (see also *Mafan*).

Wo yao This phrase means 'I want' and, although it sounds demanding, aggressive and not particularly polite, this is not necessarily the case. If you can identify specifically exactly what you want or need, you'll be more likely to get it. Staff in all kinds of outlets in the PRC are more likely to say *meiyou* (see above) if they don't know exactly what you mean. Similarly, *bu yao* or 'Don't want' sounds rude but, with a smile and *xie xie*, it's quite acceptable.

Xie xie The phrase meaning, 'Thank you'.

Zai jian Literally, 'See you later' or 'Goodbye'. Perhaps because of the importance of *guanxi*, there is no word for 'Goodbye' without it meaning 'See you later'.

Zhou san A Cantonese phrase that combines 'Hello' with 'Have you had your lunch yet?', and should only be used before lunch.

Bibliography

Sun Zi, illustrated by Tsai Chih Ching. *The Art of War.* AsiaPac Comic Series, Asiapac Books, Singapore, 1991.

Beijing Scene Guidebook. Beijing Scene Publishing, Beijing. Published annually.

Beijing Scene. Beijing Scene Publishing, Beijing. Periodical published bi-weekly.

Business China. Economist Intelligence Unit. Periodical published bi-weekly, Hong Kong.

China Business: The Portable Encyclopedia for Doing Business in China. Series editor, Edward G. Hinkelman. World Trade Press, San Rafael, California, 1995.

Kristof, N. & Wudunn, S. *China Wakes.* Vintage Books, New York, 1995.

Yang Liyi. *100 Chinese Idioms and Their Stories.* Commercial Press, Hong Kong, 1987.

Bibliography

Zhang Ciyun. *Chinese Idioms and Their Stories*. Beijing Foreign Languages Press, 1996.

Bonavia, D. *The Chinese: a portrait*. Penguin Books, London, 1982.

Sinclair, K. & Wong Po-yee, I. *Culture Shock!* Graphic Arts Center Publishing Co., Portland, 1990.

Tsao Hsueh-Chin & Kao Ngo. *The Dream of Red Mansions*. Beijing Foreign Languages Press, Beijing, 1994.

Cradock, P. *Experiences of China*. John Murray, London, 1994.

From Emperor to Citizen: the autobiography of Pu Yi. Beijing Foreign Languages Press, Beijing, 1989.

Schneiter, F. *Getting Along with the Chinese*. Asia 2000, Hong Kong, 1992.

Campbell, N. Manchester Business School Research Paper, *European Expatriates in China, The Inside Story*. China Research Unit, Manchester Business School, Manchester, 1996.

Xiao Mao & Nan-tze. *The Man With The Key Is Not Here*. Pacific Venture Press, Hong Kong, 1990.

Pan Ling. *Old Shanghai: Gangsters in Paradise*. Heinemann Asia, Singapore, 1984.

Hong Yingming, illustrated by Tsai Chih Chung. *The Roots of Wisdom*. AsiaPac Comic Series, Asiapac Books, Singapore, 1991.

Luan Baoqun. *Tales About Chinese Emperors*. Hai Feng Publishing, Hong Kong, 1994.

Melvin, S. *The US–China Business Council: Guide to Training*. US–China Business Council, Washington, 1996.

Index

Index